THE BEST
WOMEN'S STAGE
MONOLOGUES
OF 1991

JOCELYN A. BEARD has edited The Best Men's Stage Monologues of 1990, The Best Women's Stage Monologues of 1990, One Hundred Men's Stage Monologues from the 1980's, One Hundred Women's Stage Monologues from the 1980's, and has co-edited The Best Stage Scenes for Men from the 1980's and The Best Stage Scenes for Women from the 1980's.

JOSEPHINE ABADY is the Artistic Director of the Cleveland Playhouse in Cleveland, Ohio.

Other Books for Actors from Smith and Kraus

The Best Men's Stage Monologues of 1990

The Best Women's Stage Monologues of 1990

Street Talk: Character Monologues for Actors

Great Scenes for Young Actors From the Stage

The Best Stage Scenes for Men from the 1980's

The Best Stage Scenes for Women from the 1980's

One Hundred Men's Stage Monologues from the 1980's

One Hundred Women's Stage Monologues from the 1980's

The Great Monologues from the Humana Festival

The Best Men's Stage Monologues of 1991

If you require pre-publication information about upcoming Smith and Kraus monologue collections, scene collections, technique books and directories, you may receive our semi-annual catalogue, free of charge, by sending your name and address to Smith and Kraus Catalogue, P.O. Box 10, Newbury, VT 05051.

THE BEST WOMEN'S STAGE MONOLOGUES OF 1991

Edited By
Jocelyn A. Beard

SK
A Smith and Kraus Book

A Smith and Kraus Book
Published by Smith and Kraus, Inc.

Copyright © 1992 by Smith and Kraus, Inc.
All rights reserved

Cover and text design by Jeannette Champagne

Manufactured in the United States of America

First Edition: January 1992
10 9 8 7 6 5 4 3 2 1

Publisher's Cataloging in Publication
(Prepared by Quality Books Inc.)

The best women's stage monologues of 1991/Jocelyn A. Beard.
p. cm.
Includes bibliographical references.
ISBN 1-880399-01-6

1. Monologues. 2. Acting. I. Beard, Jocelyn A.
PN4307.M6   808.8245

91-66288

Smith and Kraus, Inc.
Main Street, P.O. Box 10, Newbury, Vermont 05051
(802) 866-5423

ACKNOWLEDGMENTS

Grateful thanks to the playwrights and their agents. Jocelyn A. Beard would also like to thank Kevin Kitowski for his love and support.

CONTENTS

CONTENTS

CONTENTS

x

FOREWORD

After reading through practically everything that was produced in the 1991 season, I have but one word of advice for my sisters in theater: Get ready! The 1990's are already replete with the artistic breakthroughs hinted at in the 80's, and women's roles are choicer than ever.

Thanks to the tireless efforts by repertory theaters to provide playwrights and actors with environments in which theater may be pushed right to the cutting edge, 1991 has presented us with great plays and roles; and women are at last being presented in places outside the home, office and park bench. In Richard Lay's *Sparky's Last Dance*, we travel to death row where we meet Nancy and Lily, two women contemplating life on the eve of their executions. The psychotic Lorraine in Sam Henry Kass's *Lusting After Pipino's Wife*, likes to pick up hunters in diner parking lots. Courageous Javalene of Sherry Coman's *Say Zebra*, risks her life to travel to South Africa to investigate the disappearance of her best friend, and finally, we meet the outrageous Glad Aggy, a woman who spends her life perfecting the fine art of fibbing in Terri Wagener's *The Tattler*.

In 1991 we meet women who cope with violence, perpetrate violence, battle the Inquisition in 14th Century France, deal with a brain-damaged brother, find passion in the hills of Appalachia, contend with the loneliness of middle age, and remember life as a slave in Mississippi. As you go through this book I think you will agree that this final decade before we have to switch over to a new millennium promises to be an exciting time in theater history.

Start memorizing!

—Jocelyn A. Beard
Patterson, NY
Winter, 1991

INTRODUCTION

From my perspective, the great value of the audition monologue (and, I suspect, the source of much resistance and fear) is that it invites you (indeed, <u>requires</u> you) to acknowledge your own uniqueness and to work with a strong and clear sense of its power. This about it: what better opportunity do you have to show a director who you are, what moves you to feeling and action, where your passion lives? If you're an actor who truly understands this, then you know that there's no right or wrong way with a monologue, that what a director wants most to see is <u>you</u>, and that a well chosen monologue, truthfully and imaginatively presented, offers you a valuable chance to reveal and express yourself.

That begins with your choice of audition pieces. Your selections speak volumes about your imagination and originality, and I must say that it helps enormously if you surprise me. The fact is, if you choose pieces I haven't heard before, you are virtually guaranteed to receive my full attention. I needn't tell you then that's a very important first step. And not an easy one, because (let's face it) there's still no surfeit of great roles out there for women. But the monologues collected in this volume will go far to aid you in that respect. They are drawn from works by some of our most exciting and forward-thinking contemporary writers; they are spoken by some of the richest and most passionately conceived characters you will ever encounter; they will challenge your intellectual and emotional resources alike; and they will require you to make aggressive, thoughtful choices.

I believe very strongly in seeking work that engages us completely. This is more important than ever, especially if what so many of my actor friends say is true—that nowadays the roles they are offered rarely allow them to express themselves fully. Well, I agree that in many respects the theatrical climate is chillier than ever, affecting not only the numbers of play being produced but also the <u>kinds</u> of plays. Depth isn't exactly the first thing on a lot of people's minds these days. So it's crucial for all of us in the theatre to remember that we are artists, and that we are obliged to commit

INTRODUCTION

ourselves entirely to whatever resources we command. Now I'm not so idealistic as to claim that by working on audition monologues you will find the one true path to creative enlightenment. But I am asking you as responsible theatre artists to let your auditions engage you, to regard them not as necessary evils but as real opportunities for self-expression, as chances to act.

If you share my feelings (and it's in my interest to believe you will; after all, I am in the business of producing and directing plays) then I think you'll find this volume of great value. The editor has adventurous taste and a sensitive ear for authentic voices that speak to the hearts of women everywhere. So read well, work hard, trust your uniqueness, and surprise us always.

—Josephine Abady
Artistic Director
Cleveland Playhouse
Cleveland, Ohio

THE BEST
WOMEN'S STAGE
MONOLOGUES
OF 1991

ABUNDANCE
by Beth Henley
Wyoming Territory - 1860's - Macon Hill (20's)

Macon sees a young woman sitting on a bench outside a stagecoach station. She stops to speak to her.

(Macon Hill enters wearing goggles and a cape. She is covered with road dust and carries a satchel and green biscuits on a platter. She is whistling. She stops when she sees Bess.)

MACON: Lord Almighty.

[BESS: What?]

MACON: You're like me.

[BESS: Huh?]

MACON: Sure. You're like me. Biscuit?

[BESS: Please.]

MACON: Go ahead. Help yourself. What's mine is yours; what's yours is mine. After all, you're like me. You've come out west to see the elephant. Hey, true or no?

[BESS: Elephant. No.]

MACON: To see what's out there; whatever's out there. *(Beat.)* What do you guess is out there?

[BESS: Don't know.]

MACON: [Right.] Could be anything. I savor the boundlessness of it all. The wild flavor. I'm drunk with western fever. Have you ever seen a map of the world?

[BESS: Uh huh.]

MACON: Well, it stopped my heart. There are oceans out there. Oceans aplenty, and I swear to you I'm gonna see one and walk in one and swim in one for sure. I love water, it never stops moving. I want to discover gold and be rich. I want to erect an ice palace and kill an Indian with a hot bullet. I'm ready for some sweeping changes. How about you? We could be friends throughout it all. It's part of our destiny. I can smell destiny. One day I'm gonna write a novel about it all and put you in it. What's your name?

1

AMATEURS
by Tom Griffin
New England - Present - Jennifer Collins (30's)

At a party, Jennifer tells Nathan about her brief attempt at a career as an actress in Hollywood.

JENNIFER: Excited, Nathan? I was ecstatic! I was already planning my wardrobe for the Emmys, already thinking about how in a few weeks, I'd have my own parking space, my own little table in the commissary. Maybe my own stupid custom-designed trailer. All that...stuff. And so I read one more time. My third callback. But, I didn't get it. What's the saying? "Close only counts in horseshoes." Right, Wayne? Well, that's what I was. Close. I went outside. It was one of those hazy L.A. days, one of those days when everything felt so hot and...artificial. I could see the Hollywood sign shimmering up in the hills. So I got in my rented Plymouth and drove up to Lake Hollywood. Lake Hollywood, it's perfect! The goddamn thing is made of concrete. I walked around it. And all I could think about was, "Are there fish in this lake?" So I asked somebody. I actually went up to this guy, this worn down looking middle-aged guy, and I said, "Are there fish in this lake?" You know what he said? "This is Hollywood, lady. No fish except for the sharks. No bottom except for the slime. No princes except for the frogs." And we both laughed.
[NATHAN: How ... cynical.]
JENNIFER: *(Giving Nathan a look.)* I left about two weeks later. I didn't have the guts. It wasn't the talent. It was the guts.

2

Alvin and Karen have recently met on their adjoining balconies.
Alvin is neurotic to the extent of barely being able to leave his
apartment. Karen gives him some commiseration and advice.

KAREN: Alright. I know. I've got my own problems. Who am
I to give advice, right?

[ALVIN: Right.]

(A beat.)

KAREN: I'm going to do it anyway. I understand what you said
about traffic and noise and pushy people and I agree. There are
some real losers out there. I don't enjoy them. Who does? But
they exist and you have to deal with it. Get yourself a system.
Defend yourself, damnit! Figure out a way to walk among those
bastards and survive.

[ALVIN: Hmmmmmmm.]

KAREN: I know what you're talking about, Alvin, believe me.
There is no such thing as please and thank you and excuse me anymore. Hey! The last time I saw a movie there were these two guys
sitting in front of me talking. I asked them very nicely to be quiet.
This one guy turns around and tells me to eat shit. That's what he
said. I couldn't believe it. I was shocked. There is this tree outside
my building that I love. I like to eat my lunch there when the
weather's nice. Now, it smells like pee and I won't go near it.
People are peeing on my tree! A woman took my parking space the
other day. I was waiting for another car to leave. Must have been
ten minutes. Finally it pulls out and this woman whips right in and
takes my space. Just took it. I was furious. She gets out and I

3

say, "Excuse me, I was waiting for that space." Didn't even look my way. She knew what she did and couldn't have cared less. I know, Alvin. I know how you feel. I wanted her dead. *(On a roll now.)* You know that statue in Sheridan Park? The one with that soldier on a horse?

[ALVIN: That's General Sheridan.]

(Small beat.)

KAREN: [Oh. *(Recognizes the logic.)* Oh. Well, anyway...] Someone has spray painted the horse's... *(Indicating the horse's crotch.)* THINGS...pink. I don't know why people do these things. Everything is falling apart and I don't get it either, but they won't keep me from seeing a movie. I'll find another parking space. The statue will be cleaned...

[ALVIN: What about your tree?]

KAREN: [I'll find another one.] See? You gotta blow it off. Roll with it.

[ALVIN: Roll with it?]

KAREN: Whatever works for you, Alvin. Don't give up your life. Don't get chased into your apartment. If you do, you lose.

BEATRICE
by Ian Brown
A French village - 14th Century - Beatrice (40's)

After spending many years in a dark little cell, Beatrice is finally released by the Inquisition, who tried her for witchcraft. She must tell her story to the villagers in hopes that they will forgive her the crime of having had an affair with a priest and allow her to live out the rest of her life in peace. Years of confinement with no one to speak to have left their mark on Beatrice, who tends to ramble. Here, she speaks of her daughters and of her love for them.

BEATRICE: I worship the Virgin, adore her. She speaks to God for women. She is the God of women. Not just an angel interceding. She saves us herself. They told me that this was heresy too. If it's heresy, it's heresy to a man, not to a woman. Why should the Virgin not be our God? She's the woman of women, the mother of mothers. She understands us. She brings life. She brings children.

My daughters used to de-louse me. I love it when my daughters de-louse me. That's when we relax, when they tell me their hopes. It was at de-lousing when they were younger that they told me their hopes about marriage and I told them about pleasure and men and disappointment.

I kept their first menstrual blood. I preserved the blood of their first bleeding, the blood that marks them a woman, to make a love potion later so that their husbands would love them. It's a charm a woman with her daughters in her heart has to use so that the husbands keep her daughters in their hearts. How men hit women! They lose their tempers. They're used to being in command. But if a man cares, he won't hit a woman. A lot of men beat women in the way of things, without thinking. They expect them to do what they're told, no arguments. Some don't. Pierre didn't hit me, even though we were lovers.

5

BEATRICE

None of my men hit me. Except my first husband. Orthon, my second, might have, but I was older then: I had my own strength in age and riches. If the charm can save my daughters from being beaten by their men, then you must use it. Even if it is sorcery, which it isn't.

When the bleeding came to Condors, I looked her straight in the eye and asked what was worrying her. She told me. I told her what being a woman means and how things might be. A mother must do that. I did it for all my girls. We knew that as soon as she started to bleed, we must look round for a husband for her.

If you have riches and power, you marry for riches and power. Love isn't a question. You make a business arrangement for your family. I had the dowry. I had the little wealth we owned and I wanted my daughters to be safe. They would say things like, "Why have I got to marry him? He's horrible!" Well, Condors did anyway. He isn't good looking, her husband, I'll give you that, but he is steady and he has a manor and he doesn't drink and they say he didn't beat his first wife—she died in childbirth, poor thing—and he doesn't beat Condors. There you are, if there was anything I could do to help make Condor's life more, well, pleasant, of course I did it. That's why I kept the blood to make the right love potion for them all. And perhaps Ava has trouble with a husband who chases all the time after whores, but there's nothing wrong with an open business transaction and he doesn't keep her or the children short. And he doesn't beat her. She just feels humiliation that he's so open about it. But what can you do about it? What can you ever do? He's never brought her disease. And Condors is settled with her ugly man and they are almost friends. He's gentle. My potion really worked for him. And Esclarmonde's husband takes proper care of her even if he does like a drop of drink. And Phillipa, my favourite, red haired like me. Her husband is kind. He only hits her in anger. And only once in a while. He does care about her.

6

BEATRICE

So perhaps my potions have worked. Without them, things would have been worse. And they don't starve, my girls. They all have prestige and position. My grandchildren are all well enough off and healthy, thanks be to the Virgin.

My daughters are my joy. This, I tell you, is what matters to me, even more than my home. They stood by me. Full of tears, they were. Oh well. The Cathars always say that the souls of the dead, the good souls go through the holes in a woman's body into the body of the unborn child. So a soul never dies, it just moves on to the next body. That's why my girls are so good. When Pierre told me this, I always said that, if the good souls went into a baby's body, why couldn't it talk when it came out. He never had an answer. But my daughters have good souls in them. They always had. They've been good to me. I suppose all my men have used me in the end. But my daughters spoke for me.

BETSEY BROWN
A Rhythm and Blues Musical
by Ntozake Shange and Emily Mann
St. Louis - 1959 - Betsey (12)

On her way to school, young Betsey fantasizes about life and marriage.

BETSEY:
Mama, I been thinking—
when I get married I could be
Mrs. Cora Sue Betsey Ann Calhoun-Brown-Eisenhower
I could marry the President
or maybe even Duke Ellington
Mrs. Cora Sue Betsey Ann Calhoun-Brown-Eisenhower
if one of them died
I could marry Willy Earl from the 8th grade
but he's so colored and got no manners
no—I'ma stick with Eisenhower or Ellington
Oh, but what about Sugar Ray Robinson
I'd still have my career like you
an intellectual
why didn't you marry W. E. B. DuBois
who's not so dark as Daddy
And a intellectual on top of that
more your type
but then, I like my Daddy.
If I marry the President I shall call
Willy Earl and everybody
and invite them all
to a big party for the colored folks
in Little Rock, Arkansas
with bar-b-que and cannons and lots of root beer
just for the colored
I'll do that next year
I'm Miss Cora Sue Betsey Ann Calhoun-Brown

BETSEY BROWN

soon to be married to a Negro man of renown.
There's Cab Calloway, Machito, Dizzy Gillespie
Tito Puente, Col. Davis, Nasser, James Brown...
Then I'd be Mrs. Brown-Brown
Oh, no, that won't do.
I know who I'll marry!!!!
I'll marry *Nkruma*.

BETSEY BROWN
A Rhythm And Blues Musical
by Ntozake Shange and Emily Mann
St. Louis - 1959 - Betsey (12)

Betsey's mother has left her father and here, Betsey longs for her return.

BETSEY: *(spoken)*
I wonder, do all children search the sky
for answers to wishes?
I think, maybe—I don't know—I could like Carrie
but...
I wish: Mama would come home,
singing and happy, snapping her fingers
and making all the time she was away,
just disappear.
We'd never have to remember
how much we miss her.
I wish Daddy would stay home
and never go to work,
never go to meetings,
make us dinner and play games
and take us to the ball game
and to see Art Blakey and Ike and Tina Turner
and Mama would come, too,
and just laugh and laugh
and no one would cry or fight
or be stormin' around
or act all tense
like they wanted to put some claws on they hands
and just tear you all up...
I wish Mama would just appear like nothin's happened
and cuddle with me
and tell me her secrets
and all she's been thinkin'
like always...
I wish Mama would come home [and like Carrie...]

10

BLOOD ISSUE
by Harry Crews
Rural Georgia - Present - Mabel (70's)

At an explosive family reunion, Mabel is forced to confront her
past by the persistant questioning of her younger son, Joe, who
has long suspected that his mother was keeping a secret from the
family. It seems that when it was proved that Mabel's husband,
Frank, was incapable of fathering a child, Mabel and Frank
turned to their best friend, Lonny, who became the biological
father of their children. Here, Mabel wanders the house on a
sleepless night, remembering Frank and Lonnie, both now dead,
and her love for them.

MABEL: *(Singing.)* Was you there when they crucified my Lord/
was you there when they crucified my Lord/oh Lord/it set the world
a tremble, tremble, tremble/was you there when they crucified my
Lord.

*(A small lamp comes on at a table by the shelf of knick-knacks and
pictures, lighting the stage dimly, showing MABEL in a long white
night gown. She takes her hand from the switch of the lamp and lifts
it to let it rest on the black panther. Over all of this she has
continued to sing.)*

Was you there when they spierced him in the side/was you there
when they spierced him in the side/oh Lord/it set the world a
tremble, tremble, tremble/was you there when they spierced him in
the side.

*(Her voice finally fades to silence on the chorus, but the grieving
blues guitar continues for maybe a minute and then it too fades and
dies.)*

God, Frank with that guitar and Lonny singing. All gone now.
Gone forever. Well, we made it the best we could. The only way

11

we known how to make it. Let them that's settin down marks agin us or settin down marks for us, set'm down. We had what we had. *(She strokes the panther.)* Lonny bout busted his britches when he won his painther. And Frank too, proud as if he'd a won it hisself. By rights he should a won it. By rights he should a...should a...by rights. *(Her voice has been soft, gentle but now even more gently.)* By rights. *(More harshly.)* To hell with rights! Rights ain't never fed me and rights ain't never kept me warm.

(She moves away from the panther and picks up a picture farther down the shelf. Gentle laughter.)

First house we ever called ourn. No queen ever thought her palace was purtier. And Frank and Lonny built it with nothin but gut and grunt.

(A recliner that has been sitting with its back to her and to the audience moves almost imperceptibly, so tiny a movement at first that any of the audience that has seen it wonders did it really move. During what follows, though, the recliner moves again, swiveling, coming slowly around, until Joe is revealed sitting in the diffused light watching his mother who is facing the shelves. Joe has a drink in his right hand resting on the arm of the recliner. So still does he sit through the entire monologue that he does not seem to be breathing.)

MABEL: *(Laughing.)* Oncet it'as finished you could smell the turpintine outen that green pine from a mile away. Godamighty, how many folks in this day and time'd even think two men could take that many trees down with a crosscut saw, much less snake'm out'n the woods with a mule an split'em with nothin but wedge and mallet? Not many I reckon. *(Pauses.)* Not many coulda or woulda done it. But they both thought I oughten to have a fitten house to have my baby in. That baby. No screens and wooden windows and

12

BLOOD ISSUE

a shotgun hall. Ten by ten rooms and one special for that baby. That baby. Les see now. What we brung to the marriage, weddin presents. Yes. A fry pan, a iron wash pot, four plates and four knives an forks and one big spoon for dippin, a iron bedstid with slats and cornshuck mattress, four quilts, four sheets. Frank and Lonny built a little cook table and a bigger table to eat offen with a bench on each side instead of chairs, a chest, a drawers, a plank ironin board wrapped in striped bed tickin an two flat irons. Yes. An the proudest thing of all, a Home Comfort, Number 8, wood stove with a hot water resevoir and four eyes on top. God of us all it was gone to be good hot water for that baby. That baby. Mis Emily didn't want me to see it. Didn't want Frank to see it. But I seen it. I held it agin me til it died and Frank held me holdin the baby and him cryin cause it wouldn't cry til it died. And Lonny helpless just standin there helpless as everbody else an finally him holdin the three of us with that baby dead amongst us. And Frank would not be comforted. Would not be comforted. Would not believe it was not some taint in his blood. Crying, the sin of my life is in my blood, tainted, all tainted. My poor sweet Frank. My poor sweet Lonny. Oh, Lonny, what can we do for Frank? With Frank. Love him. We can love him. And we did. We did. Love. Oh, God. Oh, my Savior.

BLOOD ISSUE
by Harry Crews
Rural Georgia - Present - Mabel (70's)

Mabel is under pressure from her son Joe to reveal the dark truth about her relationships with his father Frank and his father's best friend Lonny. Here, she begins to talk.

MABEL: Yeah, I meant all three of us. Close as three people could git. Lonny and Frank and me. Lonny stood up for Frank at the weddin. It was Lonny led the shiveree that night. Frank and me in a big feather bed cause it was so cold out the ground was froze. And Lonny was out there howlin and laughin and ringin a cow bell, him and the other young men of the county, bangin on pots and singin and drinkin and me and Frank like two children in that big feather bed gigglin and cuttin the fool. But some time after midnight it quieted down except for the fiddles. *(Her voice has gone dreamy.)* Them fiddles sweet as angels. Then after some long time—or maybe it weren't so long—it's hard to know when Lonny started singin, his voice comin right in with the fiddles, so pretty and so soft it was in the fiddles before you ever known he'd commenced to sing. When Lonny was a young man he could sing the birds right out of the trees. A voice that went right into you bones and stayed there til you whole body was quick with it. *(Catching herself up, almost as if being startled from sleep.)* That big fool! It was him that put everbody up to setting Frank's wagon on top of the house. *(Laughter that is a little forced from having to turn from the beauty of Lonny's voice.)* Frank come out of the house next mornin and there was his wagon straddlin the house with the shaves tied to the chimley, but Lonny showed up just like magic and we all eat the first breakfast I cooked as a wife, laughin and jokin, them pokin fun at my biscuits, and then Lonny helped Frank get his wagon down. Them two!

BREAKING UP
by Michael Cristofer
New York City - Present - She (20's-30's)

She has just met a man she thinks she likes and is talking to a friend about him on the telephone.

SHE: ...Well, he's nice. Yeah. He's...you know, he's okay. I don't know him very well. Oh, a few weeks. Well, three, four— about a month, a month and a half. So, how have *you* been? Uh-huh. Yeah. Well, it was funny seeing you like that. Well, how often do you run into people at the Statue of Liberty? How often do you go to the Statue of Liberty at all? No, we were just fooling around, you know and then, I don't know, there we were. And then there you were. Yeah. Yeah. Yeah, she was cute. Yeah, who is she? Uh-huh. Uh-huh. Uh-huh. Yeah. Oh. Uh-huh. Oh. That's nice. Yeah. Yeah, she seemed real nice. Yeah. That's great. Is this serious? Come on, I'm kidding. Okay. Okay.

Well, it was nice to see you. Yeah. Who? Me? Him? No. Not serious. No. Just...He speaks French. So it's great for me. No. He's American.

I don't know *what* he does. Well, I mean, I don't know. He goes to the gym a lot. Yeah. You can tell, can't you? Very serious. Three times a week and aerobics every day in between. Vitamins? Are you joking? He has a separate suitcase for them. Well, vitamins, minerals, amino acids, anti-oxidents. No. No pills, they're all powders. He mixes them. His kitchen looks like a laboratory. He's got everything except a Bunsen burner. No, seriously. When I first met him I thought he was on drugs, he kept popping things into his mouth. I thought he was a junkie. Turns out, it was bran. Bran. Yeah. And he has this doctor that shoots him up with vitamin C every few weeks. I went with him once. He plugs in an IV and then this guy, this doctor, plays the piano and talks to him about Kant and Velikovsky and Zen banking and...

BREAKING UP

(She laughs) It's funny, I know. He has everything done to him—manicures, pedicures, facials, high colonics...There isn't one part of his body that somebody doesn't do something to at least once a day. Well, he has this schedule. Yeah. So even if he wanted to work, he doesn't have time.

Well, he has money. He keeps going to Switzerland to check on some buildings and get his blood changed.

I shouldn't say all this. It's not fair. Well, I like him. I do. Because I can see what he's doing. Fighting. Fighting hard. Growing old. He's fighting it. And when we're together, just the two of us, I don't know...He holds on. He likes life. He wants it. He fights for it. He's selfish. Dishonest. I think he lies to me. He's not very bright. He thinks he has talent, but he doesn't. And he's sort of funny looking. But he loves life. It's sort of amazing in this day and age. And it's contagious. To be with somebody like that. He loves living. Isn't that amazing?

CHARGE IT, PLEASE
by Carlos Gorbea
Sak's Fur Dept., NYC - Present - Mrs. Howard (40-50)

Here, a woman who has devoted her life to the fine art of shopping reveals the genesis of her vocation.

MRS. HOWARD: What do I do? Why hon, I'm a shopper. I shop!

[JUANITA: How wonderful.]

MRS. HOWARD: I'm proud of it.

[JUANITA: I realized that too one day; that I had to go out and get lots of credit and start charging.]

MRS. HOWARD: It happened to me too. I remember it as if it were yesterday. I was sitting by Wallace Warner out at the pool, my husband, you know, at our little ol' ranch in Texas; he was reading the newspaper and I was sipping some bourbon, and I was thinking, trying to understand why I felt so unhappy most of the time. I mean, I felt like I wasn't worth anything, that I didn't matter in the world and Wallace Warner being so busy and all, I hardly ever saw him. I kept reading in the newspapers about all the trouble our economy was having, sweet people losing their jobs, sweet little children not getting enough to eat, and all because people in this country weren't doing enough buying. I mean how in the ding-dong is business in this country gonna keep goin' if we don't purchase those products and keep 'em movin' off those shelves? It doesn't matter if you can't afford it. Great horned toads, what the blazes is a credit card for? I know you understand me, sugar.

[JUANITA: I love you, Mrs. Howard.]

MRS. HOWARD: [Well aren't you cute.] So I was sitting by the pool there, sipping my bourbon, when suddenly all of this hit me; like a lightning bolt. I realized the only times I was happy, the only times I felt like a person, were the times I was out shopping. So I leapt up to my feet and I said, "Wallace Warner, Wallace Warner, I'm goin' shopping." Then he said, "Sure, Passion Flower, about when can I expect you home?", and I said, "Oh, in about twenty to thirty years."

[JUANITA: And what did he say then?]

MRS. HOWARD: He didn't say anything. He didn't move, he didn't put down his newspaper, he didn't bat an eyelash. I interpreted that as a sign; a sign that I was doin' the right thing. So I packed some of my best clothes, gave the dog away and I took off straight to Beverly Hills and Rodeo Drive, a place where a woman with a purpose can accomplish something.

THE CLOSER
by Willy Holtzman
New York City - Present - Iris (30-40)

Iris is puzzled when Howard, her ex-husband, invites her to dinner. As they discuss their young son and his problems, Iris is struck by Howard's inability to understand how difficult life has become for her since their divorce. Here, she describes a typical week in her new life.

IRIS: This is my week, Howard. I leave the office at three. I race home to greet Sam's 3:50 bus. He could probably manage himself, but I'm not big on latch-key parenthood. We hang out together. Baseball practice Tuesday, games Friday. Piano Wednesday. Dinner, every night. Provided there's minimal procrastination with homework, there is a session with aliens and deathrays at the computer. Goodnight, Sam. Glass of wine. Laundry. Pick up the house. Make lunch—peanut butter and banana, Wonder bread, crust on. Second glass of wine. Review the latest spread sheets. Pay bills. Rip through a few pages of some trashy paperback. Goodnight Iris. To bed. To bus. To work. Brace yourself for the sisterly pity, "How are you holding up, hon? You're so brave." Convince yourself that the hot shot just in from the branch office is not measuring your back for footprints now that word is out you cut to three-quarters time. Contemplate what Moorehouse means when he says, "I've had my eye on you for awhile." Grab a bite of the gourmet desk-side sandwich you prepared for yourself only to taste peanut butter, bananas and Wonder Bread. Wonder how Sam will explain alfalfa sprouts and brie to his skateboard cronies. Walk out of a crucial meeting mid-sentence because the little hand is on the three and Moorehouse's big hand has brushed yours twice reaching for coffee. Home again, home again, jiggedy jig. And the pathetic irony is it's all virtually indistinguishable from how it was before. Now I notice.

THE CLOSER
by Willy Holtzman
New York City - Present - Iris (30-40)

When Howard reveals that his new apartment is, in fact, the very place to which he used to bring the women he slept with while they were still married, Iris reveals a recent experience in which her own morality was put to the test.

IRIS: [You bought this place. You brought the road home. I didn't throw you out. You were already gone.]
(beat)
Do you want to know why I was late this evening? Are you interested? I got to the front door. The doorman greeted me, I had to go back out again.
(CC enters the room, crosses to the window)
I walked around the block to my old building. You can't really see the apartment from the street. The window looks onto dead space, an air shaft. But the bathroom has quite a view. Were you aware of that? A half window with pebbled glass, painted a crack from shut—a panoramic view. Downtown, uptown, the park. This place. At just the right angle, you could see a sliver of this place. It wasn't much to see. But that night you came up, that first night, afterwards, I came into the bathroom, switched off the light, and watched buildings. Windows in buildings. Sat and sat. Very contentedly. Imagined the lives on the other side of those windows. I had this sensation of invisibility—to see but not be seen. It brought me peace. I did that quite a lot.
(beat)
Last week, wonder of wonders, Bancroft the bimbo belatedly discovered that a spread sheet also refers to something besides hotel rooms and got pink-slipped, which meant an opening for marketing director. That was my job. It always was, even before she mini-skirted her way into it. But when I asked Moorehouse, he said I would have been an automatic choice, but with the reduced hours, it was a tough call. I pointed out that I had reduced lunch and cock-

THE CLOSER

tails, not work. He said lunch and cocktails were work. I said I wanted the job. He said what about my current family status? What about travel? I said I would make arrangements. He said there's a national sales conference coming up—what about that? I made arrangements.

(beat)

You should've seen me. I knocked them on their butts. I had all the answers. I was smart. I was tough. I was charming. I was funny at cocktails, at dinner. And after dinner...I was in Moorehouse's room. I was in the bathroom. There was no view. Not even a window. But mirrors. Mirrors everywhere. A view of me. The lights are so harsh, so specific. My blouse is off, my skirt. And my underwear—this would have been laundry night—I have on my jogging bra and a pair of Sam's Fruit of the Looms. What a sight. And I'm stuck. What is the procedure here? The protocol? Am I doing this right? Is this how it's done? All these mirrors, you see yourself from the front, from behind, from every angle. And what greets the eye—Jesus, the hours of exercise you thought would hold back time—the flesh presses at the elastic. The thighs dimple. Your breasts just hang there. The underwear is on the floor. And suddenly in this windowless bathroom, you feel exposed. You're sure people can see in, but you can't see out. They can see everything. The spread, the sag, the settle of you. And the space, inside. They can see that with perfect clarity. How alone you are.

(CC exits in shadow)

I came back to your door tonight, nodded at the doorman. Came up the elevator expecting to see God-knows-what—ghosts. Then you. And this. I was going to give everything back, the trinkets, the trophies, even the wedding band. Wipe the slate clean. And if you were repentant, reformed, if you were very good, I was going to take you back. For Sam, I told myself. Because you...I...we are fucking him up. The phone...the little red light was on. Where the hell was I? Alone in somebody's bathroom. [And you were, where?]

THE COLORADO CATECHISM
by Vincent J. Cardinal
Rehab center in Colorado - Present - Donna (30's)

Donna is a woman struggling to overcome her alcoholism in order to regain custody of her young son. At the rehab center, she finds herself drawn to Ty, an artist and fellow addict. Here, Donna tells Ty the sad tale of her senior prom.

DONNA: I wanted to go to Prom.

[TY: I would listen and shake.]

DONNA: The day before prom, I got a note in my locker that said...

[TY: and she'd talk.]

DONNA: "Dearest Donna, Will you go to the prom with me?"

[TY: And I'd vomit. And she'd talk. She was always there.]

DONNA: "Love, Jean-Marc."

He was the most beautiful boy in the world. I got that note and I cut my afternoon classes and I went home and I got a tall glass of milk, and a bag of Oreos, and got in my bed and watched the Prize Movie on Channel Forty Three, all afternoon. I was beautiful with Oreos in my bed and Jean-Marc in my head.

My mother helped me make my own dress, a strapless top that fit real tight and then swooshed out at the bottom, and Mama spent twenty dollars on my hair-do and nails. I said I was sure Jean-Marc was the kind of boy who would buy a wrist corsage for his prom date, so Mama gave me her silver bracelet—that Daddy had given her—for my other wrist. That night I posed for pictures all dressed up in my prom clothes and I waited by the window, and I waited at the end of the drive way and I waited at the top of the street. But it was a joke all along. I knew that note wasn't real. The hand writing was just too girlie. But I couldn't go back home, because I knew Mama would be disappointed in me. So, I walked to the baseball diamond and sat down in the bleachers until I could go home and pretend I had been to Prom.

I told my Johnny, my husband, that I'd fall in love with the man who gave me a wrist corsage and you know what he did? He said, "I'll kill the S.O.B. that gives my woman a corsage." [Ty, you okay?]

¿DE DÓNDE?
by Mary Gallagher
American Southwest - Present - Lillian (50's)

Here, Lillian—a nun who has devoted her life to providing shelter for refugees from El Salvador—explains her motivation to a younger sister.

LILLIAN: Listen, I was sixteen when I joined the convent. They trained me as a nurse, and they sent me to this hospital in Louisiana—a whites-only hospital, except the aides were black. But that really didn't sink in, until one day an aide got sick, and she fainted, and I picked her up, this black woman, and put her in a bed. Well, they bounced me out of Louisiana pretty quick. And I started seeing how things go—not just there—everywhere. And ever since, I've just seen more and more and gotten madder. See what I'm saying here?

[KATHLEEN: I guess...]

LILLIAN: It had to be done. She fainted, I was there. You don't go looking for it—it's what's presented to you. Hey, I've lived in this Valley almost all my life. But up till 1980, I'd never even met anybody from El Salvador. They just didn't come here. I came back to this house to take care of my father, 'cause he was old and getting sick. And then in 1980, all hell broke loose down there, and all of the sudden, all these Salvadorans were sleeping in my yard. So I started bringing 'em inside. And pretty quick, we had twenty at the dinner table. And my father looked at me and said, "What's going on, pal?" And I told him what I'm telling you. I might not want to do it, I might not even like it, but it's gotta be done. And I'm here. *(Pause.)* Come on inside and have a drink. Then if you still want to, yeah, you can go home.

¿DE DÓNDE?
by Mary Gallagher
A Texas courtroom - Present - Lynne (30's-40's)

Lynne, the senior partner of a Texas law firm sums up her defense of a young Salvadoran who has entered the United States illegally, and whom the INS is trying to deport.

LYNNE: Somebody said that for evil to flourish, all that's necessary is that good men do nothing. *(Beat; goes on.)* Alirio Perez is seventeen years old. But he is a good man, unable to do nothing in the face of enormous evil. If he returns to El Salvador, he will continue to speak out against the corrupt, vicious government of that so-called democracy. And he will be suppressed by the most vicious means. *(Beat; then.)* Your Honor, Mr. Perez's case is the most clearcut of any asylum case I have argued. The exhibits and affidavits, and his own moving testimony have proven beyond a doubt that he was arrested, tortured, and threatened with death for himself and his family, solely for peaceful political activities in pursuit of some small measure of dignity and freedom for the Salvadoran people. *(Beat; then.)* The Asylum Act does not require that he prove that he will be persecuted if he returns to his home country. It only requires that he have a well-founded fear of persecution. And anyone who has spent two months in the hands of the Salvadoran National Police has a fear that is well-founded. *(Beat; then.)* The greatest freedom that we have in this great country is the freedom to express our deeply-held beliefs, whether or not we support the groups in power. We cherish this freedom, and the Asylum Act is based on our desire to extend it to those who have struggled to live by its principles even in the face of terror and repression. My client has struggled in this way in his home country. Now he has come to the United States, seeking the protection of this freedom. Refusing him asylum would be saying that heroic commitment to our most cherished freedom doesn't count, when it happens in El Salvador.

THE GEOGRAPHY OF LUCK
by Marlane Meyer
Las Vegas - Present - Teddy (30's)

When Dixie, a once-famous singer, is released from prison, he returns to his home in Las Vegas where he meets Teddy, the daughter of his cellmate. Teddy and Dixie are immediately attracted to one another and spend a lot of time in Teddy's shack in the desert. Here, Teddy tells Dixie of a time she almost got married.

TEDDY: Almost got married one time, to this clown, pretty famous clown, from Mexico? People like to think that clowns are happy but he was real moody, he was always depressed. I remember this one time we were at this motel in the San Fernando Valley called the Pink Motel? Supposed to be romantic. We were taking a trial run at, you know, being together every day and it was our third day and we were celebrating...I was drinking cold duck and he was drinking Romilar P.M. and he started, screaming, about how I was killing him with my needs, or knees, I think he said knees. I have this scar on my knee that used to bug him. He hated scars, any kind of deformity. He used to ask me, didn't I think he had a perfect body? But he was small, he was always getting beat up.

So we got into this fight and he pulled out a gun and started shooting the bed and these motel creeps came and put us out of the room and we had to sleep in my car and when I woke up the next morning he was dead.

His name was Conejo. Conejo means rabbit.

GROTESQUE LOVESONGS
by Don Nigro
Terre Haute, IN - Summer 1980 - Romy (22)

When Romy's fiance, John, inherits a fortune, the two sit down to discuss their future and it soon becomes evident that John is still too young to settle down. Romy has already done all the adventuring she wants and is ready for a home and a family. Here, she describes her feelings to John.

ROMY: I was just a baby when I married Billy, and I knew I probably shouldn't devote my life to a man that still read comic books but he was like a little puppy and I couldn't say no. We had a trailer by the crick in Bloomington about the size of a dog house and all he did was drink beer and drag race and collect unemployment, and he won a bunch of races but instead of the cash prize he always took the trophies, which looked like somebody made them in manual training class in reform school. We were living on canned peaches and there was so many trophies you had to do a broad jump to get to the bathroom, and one night Billy didn't come home, and I figured that was the excuse I was looking for, so Sunday morning I was stuffing my clothes in brown paper bags when a police car pulled up, and I just knew he'd been killed in a race, but actually he was coming out of the Cootie Club with a cheerleader and a truck full of chickens ran over them. Billy loved cartoons, I thought it was right he should die like Wiley Coyote. So I filled up my Volkswagen with paper bags and started west. I wasn't even going to stop in Terre Haute to see my folks but I had to pee real bad and the car died in front of the Wabash Cigar Store and three old guys came out on the sidewalk and stared at my legs. Then I was waiting tables at the Waffle House when I met Henry, and I thought, well, at least this one's got money, but he was worse, he sold real estate and wanted to take care of me, and we had purple rugs and metal furniture and he shot small animals with a large gun and had sex with lady real estate agents with wigs and little name tags so I got the hell out of there and went back to the Waffle House

GROTESQUE LOVESONGS

and then Mr. Agajanian needed a personal secretary although for what I don't know because we'd just sit there all day in that house and his snakey eyes would always zero in on my breasts so I kept gettin up to go to the bathroom and he thought I had a kidney problem and then I met you and one morning I was late and I let myself in the house and went up the stairs and found him sitting in front of the television set staring at the farm report stiff as a carp and cold as a Dilly bar so I went back to the Waffle House and he left you all his money but you don't want to marry me and take me to the Grand Ole Opry to grow Appaloosas and what I'd really like is to live in that beautiful old house which I think was built by Dracula's uncle but sometimes Johnny I think you're even more bizarre than Pete is. Why don't you kiss me or something?

GROTESQUE LOVESONGS
by Don Nigro
Terre Haute, IN - 1980 - Romy (22)

Romy has just dropped John for his brother Pete. Confused
feelings and some incipient cold feet appear. Pete asks Romy
what she wants. Romy responds.

ROMY: *(Turning back to him, furious.)* I want to live someplace.
I want walls that don't belong to somebody else. I want wallpaper
with flowers on it, really complicated patterns. I want to bake bread
in a big kitchen on Saturdays and cut fat slices of it while it's still
warm and spread butter on it and give it to my children. I want
children. I want girls and I want boys and I want to give them
books that smell good with colored pictures. I want to read to them
in the afternoon in a rocking chair. I want a rocking chair. And I
want rose bushes, white roses and red. And trees. I want lots of
trees, no stupid son of a bitch cuts down any trees where I live.
Lilacs. Honeysuckle. Trumpet vines. I want a garden. Melons,
honeydew and watermelons and strawberries. And I want cats, house
cats, big fat ones that sleep under the piano and snore in your lap.
I want a piano. I want to learn to play the piano. I want to work
in the yard. I want a big old house where I belong and where
people need me to be there. And I want to live to be very old and
I want hundreds of grand- children. That's what I want, and I'm not
ashamed of it, and I don't care what anybody thinks about it, that's
what I want. Also I want you, but you're entirely too stupid to take
me, so too bad for you, cowboy, I'm going back to the Waffle
House.

THE HAVE-LITTLE
by Migdalia Cruz
South Bronx - 1970's - Lillian (13-15)

When Lillian discovers that she is pregnant, she becomes determined to have the baby. Despite her resolve, Lillian is often apprehensive of the future and here describes an experience on the subway that helped to bolster her confidence.

LILLIAN: Three kids came up to me in the subway today and started pulling on my purse and pushing on my belly and poking me. I was trying to get them off me and nobody helped me. It hurt me because I was so gassy. All these mens go passing by and they don't even look. And as they were pulling at me, I think "where are these boys' mothers?" I hope my baby always has his mother to tell him what to do. And then I felt somefin I never felt before—my baby turned himself full around, it was like I was walking backwards. But what an amazing thing. In my stomach, this beautiful little thing that was turning and turning. I know he wanted his mom to be okay. But more than that, I thought all of a sudden that those boys were just somebody's babies. And I looked deep into the littlest one's eyes...and a minute later, I was slapping the shit out of him. My baby turned again and it was happy because his mommy was gonna be okay. They left me alone after that. Even now, when I'm ready to pop nobody bothers. They keep away. They know I'm gonna be somebody's mommy. It's gonna be somefin.

THE HAVE-LITTLE
by Migdalia Cruz
South Bronx - 1970's - Lillian (13-15)

Lillian's mother dies at the exact moment that she gives birth to her son, leaving young Lillian alone in a demanding world. She is haunted by feelings of grief and begins smoking cigarettes as her mother did in an effort to feel closer to her. Here, Lillian describes a nightmare.

LILLIAN: I'm gonna give up smoking. I swear to God, man. This is it. They give me bad dreams. I get afraid to go to sleep 'cause I don't know what I'll see there. Last night, I saw myself poking holes in my face wif paper airplanes and then sailing them, all covered wif blood, out the window. They fly to my father's house and he thinks they're toilet paper and wipes his ass wif them. Now he's got my blood all over his face—uhn, ass, I mean. That's the worse part. The part about his ass, because, I don't know, a daughter's not supposed to see her father's ass like that.
(Pause)
And then I walk over to the zoo. I been there five thousand times and every time I go I don't see nobody and nobody talks to me, but in this dream, I see a woman who looks so much like me, I think I'm looking in a mirror. But then she starts talking to me and she don't sound like me. She's somebody else. But she's me too. I really don't understand how that could be, so I don't speak back to her so maybe she'll go away somewheres...but she don't. And then, she's standing by my favorite thing, the gorillas and she's badmouthing them. I think this is really crazy. How could anybody do a thing like that? They're so sweet. But she does, so now I know she's not me, but I'm still not sure who she is, so I let her keep talking and she follows me all around the zoo. I go to the bird house to see the flamingoes and she stands behind me on one foot trying to be one of them.
(Pause)
Maybe she din't want me to see her so she was trying to blend in.

30

THE HAVE-LITTLE

Maybe. And every place I went, she stayed real close. I'd stop at every cage and so did she. But she'd always make like she was one of them instead of a normal human. But it was in the reptile house where she really took off, talking all kinds of bullshit. I couldn't hardly unnerstan what she was saying. Especially after I threw that chicken back in. It was like she never saw a chicken back before and it was the most delicious thing she'd ever seen. And then she jumped in wif the alligators. I reached out, but not to save her—to take the cigarette out of her mouth. Shame to let a freshly lit cigarette go to waste. And I let her kill herself. I din't feel nuffin for her, I just wanted that moist filter wif her lipstick ring in my mouth. So I grab it, take a puff and start dancing, like Mami used to. I'm real happy she's dead—the woman, I mean...And that's it. I wake up.

(Pause)

Maybe it means somefin, but I don't know what. I mean, alligators? There must be easier ways...lots of ways. Maybe it was that glass of hot chocolate...Ma used to say that hot chocolate before bed gives you bad dreams.

(Long Pause)

And every night before I went to bed, she made some hot chocolate. A big glass for her and a little one for me. Everybody in my family loved it. Just now I tried to think about going to bed without it...but I couldn't. You know how it is when you get used to somefin.

I STAND BEFORE YOU NAKED
by Joyce Carol Oates
Here and Now - Woman (30's)

A woman emerging from a disasterous sexual encounter with
one of her students here reveals the feelings of loneliness and
despair which drove her into his young arms.

WOMAN: This boy named Kit—soon as I started subbing for his
class he pestered me with love, called out "Hey goodlookin" on the
street, eyeing me every chance he could, "Hey TEACH you're a
PEACH" he's got these incredible brown eyes, smooth peachy-down
skin like he hardly needed to shave, didn't look fifteen but claimed
he was seventeen which might have been true. *(Takes a deep
breath, laughs.)* So! All right, I said, all right damn you, I drove
us to this place outside town, in the woods, a motel s'posed to look
like a hunting lodge, fake logs with painted-on knotholes, I brought
along three six-packs of Coors we started drinking in the car, the
room smelled of damp and old bedclothes, somebody's hair oil or
maybe Airwick, you know the smell—*I* know the smell.
(Confidentially, to audience.) It's my strategy to praise them, oh
actually I mean every word I say, just wanted him to feel good,
y'know—good? So we're fooling around, out of breath and getting
excited, quick kisses, y'know, nervous wisecracks you roar your
head off laughing at then can't remember five minutes later. *(Makes
dancing, erotic movements, lifting arms, snapping fingers lightly.)*
"Hey let's dance, kid," I said, "y'know how to dance, huh?" and
we're falling on the bed tangling and kicking. I opened his pants
and took hold of him there but he was soft, breathing fast and
shallow like some scared animal, was he afraid? but why? of *me*?
hey why? *(Pause.)* blew in his ear and got him giggling, I teased
and said O.K. kid now's your chance, Mommy ain't anywhere near,
kissed and tickled and rubbed against him, God I was hot, my head
sort of spinning going fast like around a turn in the mountains,
Oooooooooo! hair streaming out behind me *(Lifts hair languorously
in both hands, shuts eyes.)* like it hasn't done in oh God fifteen

years. *(Pause; opens eyes.)* I was crying no I was laughing, wanted to get him hard damn it, big and hard and strong like a man, deep inside me like a man, then I'd whisper how great he was, how fantastic, make both of us feel like a million bucks, I deserve some happiness don't I, I'm a human being aren't I, not just some "sub" grateful for shitty part-time jobs—twenty-three miles I have to drive in one direction, thirty the other and never anything more than a one-year contract, Sorry that's how it is, take it or leave it Miss Snyder, tough luck. *(Grips her face with sudden violence.)* And these pouches under my eyes and a twisty look that scares the nice shy kids. And this voice in my head *Is this me? oh God—this? me? (Pause.)* But he never did get hard, it just felt like something that's been skinned, naked and velvety like a baby rabbit, he was tense and trembling like I'd hurt him or was afraid I might hurt him, finally he whispers, "I guess I don't love you, I guess I want to go home" *(Pause.)* —but I didn't even hear, I was thinking Oh fuck the beer's gonna get warm, shut my eyes seeing the road tilt and spin and the sky opening up like we're all being sucked into it— *(Pause.)* Hey let's dance kid, I said giggling, let's knock the shit out of this room, he was laughing too, maybe he was crying, nose running like a baby's and I just lay there thinking, All right kid, all right you bastards, this is it.

I STAND BEFORE YOU NAKED
by Joyce Carol Oates
Here and Now - Lady (30-50)

Here, a society matron greets the audience in the middle of her morning routine, which consists of writing checks to charitable organizations. Her isolation seems to have resulted in a poor grasp of reality which becomes increasingly more evident as she speaks.

LADY: *(Graciously.)* I am performing the
rituals
of the body I woke up in
sweet smiles writing
checks

I am the lady of the house
this house you've gazed at
from the outside   Yes
some of you have wondered
what it looks like
on the outside
Well—it *is* nice!   *(Pause.)*

Yes I am the lady of the house
this is my boudoir
I am doing what I do best
I am writing writing
POWDER BLUE CHECKS

(Pause, as SHE writes, tears check out from book, etc.)

I am "prolific"   I am much admired
I am happy to be so much   admired
as I smile smile
writing writing

I STAND BEFORE YOU NAKED

checks FLUTTER BLUE
on! In all directions!
(As if in a sudden breeze, checks flutter to floor.)

I am performing the rituals
oh! they're sac-red!
of the body I woke up in
I know *my* place
on this third-planet-from-the-sun
HEAPING RICHES LIKE GOD'S GRACE
into an emaciated face in a photograph—
Cambodian refugee no it's
is it?—Ethiopian?
SAVE THE ORPHANS FUND
SAVE THE SYMPHONY FUND
SAVE THE REDWOODS FUND

I am smiling upon you all   I'm in a good
  mood this morning
I slept well last night   and I'll sleep well
  tonight
smiling upon the FRIENDS OF THE
  MENTALLY HANDICAPPED
smiling upon the FRIENDS OF THE
  ENDANGERED YAK
smiling upon the FRIENDS OF THE
  ENDANGERED FETUS
I have many adventures   with my checkbook
I SMILE UPON ALL RACES COLORS AND
  CREEDS

(Sudden change of mood; yawns.) An—I'm a bit
  bored my poor hand is *exhausted*
(Rises from table, moves a bit stealthily.)

I STAND BEFORE YOU NAKED

Now I'll leaf through the portfolio
he keeps locked away

(LADY opens safe.)

I'll finger these sacred papers
the quarterly dividend statements   the money
  manager's reports   investments   property
  interest oh!
I suppose it's all in order, *I* wouldn't know
and—

(LADY has small pistol in palm of hand.)

—and *here!*—
which *he* keeps in the safe thinks *I* don't know
  about
I WILL HIDE IT IN MY CLOTHES

(LADY paces about the room, fantasizing, excited.)

I will cancel the FRIENDS OF THE ART
  INSTITUTE luncheon
I will attend today's Sotheby's auction
the Van Dusen estate   poor Hendrik
there is a Goya up for bidding   or is it a
  Rembrandt
Andrew Wyeth   Van Gogh   Jasper James
  oh!
one or another!
I will bid gaily and drunkenly and when
I have bought everything when
the gallery officers approach me
then I will—

I STAND BEFORE YOU NAKED

(Brandishes pistol.)

No I will buy what remains of the Hinklemann
estate
and the old Quaker cemetery north of town
I WILL TURN IT INTO A LUSH LOVELY
    MEADOW
I want sheep grazing   rail fences   inner-city
    children
I want languorous mists that linger
cow-bells and vespers and shepherds with staves
Lombardy poplars for the balmy evening breeze
if the sheep get too filthy
if the children vandalize the monuments
IF ONE OF THEM APPROACHES ME—

(Brandishes pistol.)

At the country club buffet I will   toss food onto
    the floor
I will shake the champagne bottles   FIZZLE
    SPRAY ALL OVER
I will gaze upon my lifelong friends without
    recognition
I will mutilate the ladies'   fur coats
When I am approached   when they say *Won't
you come with us*
I will smile smile smile and

(Brandishes pistol.)

No—I will park the Mercedes by a   warehouse
in my Gucci crocodile pumps I will go stumbling
through dark alleys

I STAND BEFORE YOU NAKED

when I turn my ankle   when I whimper
when one of them approaches
oh! I will run I will be terrified I will pant like a
  doe!
when one of *them* touches me
I will—
(Brandishes pistol.)

YOU THOUGHT I WAS A DEFENSELESS
WHITE LADY DIDN'T YOU...!

(Abrupt change of mood, returns to table and pen, etc.)

Oh some other   time
my migraine is
I'll cancel the luncheon though
I almost forgot the FRIENDS OF GAELIC
  they depend upon me
the FRIENDS OF THE GRAPE PICKERS   the
  FRIENDS OF THE BLIND
oh! already it's afternoon
the day will flutter by   safely

POWDER BLUE SMILES ON ALL SIDES
but—
I am crossing off my list
the COMMITTEE FOR THE PRESERVATION
  OF ST. TIMOTHY'S ABBEY
for it is chaired by a   swine
who chews
celery
noisily

(LIGHTS out.)

38

IVY ROWE
adapted by Mark Hunter and Barbara Smith
from <u>Fair and Tender Ladies</u> by Lee Smith
Appalachia - 1920's-1930's - Ivy Rowe (various ages)

Ivy, age 12, displays a remarkable talent for capturing the emotion of a moment on paper as she describes the death of her father to her teacher in a letter.

IVY ROWE:
MY DEAR MRS. BROWN:

I thank you kindly for your letter, but to answer your question, no, I do not pray. Nor do I think much of God. It is not right what he sends on people. My daddy died, to answer your question, a week ago Thursday. It was right after that big rain; you could smell spring in the air. "Go ring the bell," Momma said to Garnie, and he done so. And I could hear it ringin' ever afterwards.

(During the following, Ivy moves to the platform and carefully folds the quilt.)

I had to go help Granny Rowe undress Daddy and wash him off and put him in his good black suit and his tie. Then Granny wetted the comb and parted his hair, but Momma screamed when she seen it, said it was parted on the wrong side, so Granny changed it. Then Momma got the buryin' quilt and they wrapped him up in that; I had to wash his face. We put quarters on his eyes to keep 'em shut after they lifted him into the coffin, and Granny Rowe tied a rag under his chin to keep his mouth closed, and put a camphor cloth acrost his nose and mouth so he wouldn't turn black. And then I walked outside... *(She moves downstage again.)*

And water was runnin' everwhere; water, water, boundin' off of ever' little clift and shinin' in the sun. And the sky was as blue as a piece of cloth from the mercantile store. Buds had busted out on all the bushes and trees...It was hard walkin' in all the mud. I got it clear up to my ankles...I was cryin', too, like I couldn't hardly stop...For Daddy had loved the Spring.

IVY ROWE
adapted by Mark Hunter and Barbara Smith
from <u>Fair and Tender Ladies</u> by Lee Smith
Appalachia - 1920's-1930's - Ivy Rowe (various ages)

After losing the father of her first child in World War I, Ivy settles into married life in the Appalachian hollow of Sugar Fork. The calm of her life is disrupted by a passionate encounter with a bee man, as she describes in the following letter.

IVY ROWE: We set off on the path through the orchard, past the beegums, and commenced to climbin' Pilgrim Knob. Honey pulled his shirttail up out of his pants.

"See that rock?" I said. "My momma used to sit on that rock and cry when my daddy was so sick and things had not worked out like she thought. My momma run off with my daddy when she was fifteen..." I couldn't believe I was talkin' so much to a perfect stranger...Honey walked on ahead, his white shirt flappin' in the wind.

"And there's the blackberry thicket where Oakley and me came as kids and he kissed me for the first time." Now I was talkin' about my own husband Oakley like he was somebody I scarcely knew.

"But we're goin' this way," Honey said, steppin' off from the main trail...I felt like a girl again. I was droppin' years as I went...We came to a little bunch of scraggly pines where the trail forked again.

"That's the way to the buryin' ground," I said.

"Well, we ain't takin' that path," he said.

(She climbs up on the platform. The lights are magical.)

Now we were walkin' the top of the ridge above the treeline. Then the ridge turned flat like a meadow.

"This here is what you call a bald," Honey said. It was covered with little white flowers like stars, like a carpet of stars.

IVY ROWE

"It sure is pretty," I said. He took my hand and led me on through the flowers over onto another path which stopped at the very edge of the mountain on top of the highest cliff. For the first time I could see over the top of Bethel Mountain to another mountain, blue, purple, then mountain after mountain rollin' like the sea.

Honey dropped to the mossy ground and pulled me down beside him.

"See that hawk?" He pointed to the left and I turned my head, but when I did, he kissed me.

"Mmmmmm," he said

"What hawk?" I said.

"Mmmmmmmmm," he said.

Sugar Fork seemed far away. I laid back on the moss while he did ever'thing to me, ever'thing.

"Now do this," Honey said. *(Ivy is on her knees.)* And I did. I had never even thought of doin' such a thing before in all my life. I believe it's against the law!

Then he stretched out beside me and slept. He had gold hair all over him...I got up and walked to the edge to look out again. It was the first time I had ever been naked in the sunshine! The wind lifted my hair...Honey sat up. He said, "You look like a Princess!"

"I'm too old to be a Princess," I said.

"Then you look like a queen."

All of a sudden he made a run at me.

"Gotcha!" he called...I leaped back at him.

"Gotcha back!" I said...And we played tag there on the bald on top of Blue Star Mountain!

"Fire on the mountain, fire in the sea," Honey ran backwards, "Can't catch me!"

But I'm as big and as strong as he is, and I toppled him into the starry flowers where we laid face to face and leg to leg and toe to toe...Now he was doin' things to me with his tongue. "I reckon he goes from woman to woman like a bee goes from flower to flower," I thought. But he was the last thing left to happen to me, so it didn't bother me a bit.

"Here now," Honey said, handin' me my clothes. "We better get a move on."

"We can stay a while longer," I said. And so we did. We drank right out of a spring. We ate huckleberries and nuts and greens, and whatever Honey could catch—a rabbit, a squirrel...A white mist covered the whole world ever' mornin'...I would of stayed up there with him until I starved to death and died, I reckon, livin' on love, if he hadn't finally got tired of me, and I hadn't got sick.

"It is time," Honey said. And even tho' I cried and pitched a fit, I follered him down the mountain that mornin'.

THE LAST GOOD MOMENT OF LILY BAKER
by Russell Davis
Country inn - 1980 - Molly Kass (32)

The time is shortly after the fall of the US embassy in Tehran
and the world has become a more hostile environment for
executives abroad, provoking a deepening paranoia. Molly and
her husband are spending the weekend with friends whom they
haven't seen for some time. Molly tells about a dream she had
the previous night.

MOLLY: It was quite nasty, though, this dream. I must say.
Nasty. We were at the table downstairs and, Bob, you were pouring
wine and speaking German.

[BOB: German, really?]

[MOLLY: Yes. I was quite impressed.]

[BOB: That's funny. Speaking German.]

MOLLY: [I know.] But then Sam started speaking German too.
And then Lily. And for a while I got scared, I didn't say anything,
I thought I might be left speaking English all by myself. But when
I opened my mouth, sure enough, I spoke German too.

[BOB: German, huh? You mean we understood each other?]

MOLLY: [Oh, yes. We did.] It was wonderful. We were all quite
suddenly fluent in German.

[BOB: Yeah.]

MOLLY: The wine too. The wine got German. Mosel. And
Sam's car. I remember that was parked outside, and it turned
German. It became a Porsche. With tractor wheels. And we were
all looking out the window, commenting on Sam's new tractor
wheels. In German, of course, and Sam was telling us he was
thinking of installing a periscope. When all of a sudden Lily leaned
forward and informed us that the restaurant wasn't safe. She did. In
fact, she said the whole inn had become dangerous. The building.
Because there were other Germans outside. Real Germans roaming
around in the countryside. And these Germans, they were Nazis,
Lily said, and I remember Lily suggested we get out of there before

they arrived. So we all ran out the restaurant and out the front door. Except I didn't make it. Because I saw a bathroom, which I needed to go to. And then in the bathroom, I heard this pounding. These Germans pounding on the door. And that made me scared. Until suddenly I realized, oh, no, wait a minute. It's 1980. 1980. What are these people doing here? So I flung open the bathroom door and I screamed at these Nazis, I screamed it's 1980! You're all gone! So go away! But they didn't listen. These people, they captured me instead.

[BOB: Hmm.]

MOLLY: Then I woke up. I woke up feeling very captured.

[BOB: Yeah.]

MOLLY: Well, don't be embarrassed, Bob. It's only a dream.

[BOB: I know. Of course.]

MOLLY: I was captured, that's all. All day I've been captured. Feeling captured. I was getting especially captured downstairs. Waiting.

LOVE DIATRIBE
by Harry Kondoleon
Suburbia - Present - Sandy (20-30)

When Sandy and her brother, Orin, are paid a visit by the mysterious Frieda, they are challenged by the odd young woman to give more love in their lives. When Frieda suggests that Sandy go to the nearest hospital and tell as many strangers as possible there that she loves them, Sandy finds herself responding to the challenge. Here, Sandy returns from the hospital and relates her amazing experiences.

SANDY: Orin, I had the most extraordinary evening! You're not going to believe what happened! Oh, here's that ring to give back, take it. Where's Frieda?
(ORIN takes the ring. In response to her question, HE shrugs, wide-eyed, shell-shocked.)
SANDY: I went into the hospital and, you know, I thought, I won't chicken-out but I'd treat it like a practical joke. I went into people's rooms—no one stopped me, it was like I had a magic beam around me—and I just whispered I love you and ran out of the room. I did a whole corridor like that until I started feeling like a New Age call girl so I slowed down and followed the directions; you know, looking in their eyes, putting my hand on their chest, saying the words slowly with feeling. These old men would get erections and sit up! An old woman who was connected to all these horrible tubes sat up, pulled them all out, hugged me and said, "I love you too, darlin'!" Then I went to the children's ward where all these cancer children were crying and I went up to each one and I touched their heads and chests and eyes and I kept saying I love you and then they all stood up and we danced in a big circle laughing. *(SHE is a bit hysterical, laughing and crying with true feeling.)* Orin, I've never been so happy in my whole life!

LOVE LEMMINGS
The Very First Date of Martha Mitz
by Joe DiPietro
Here and Now - Martha (30's)

Here, an anxious divorcee assails her date with a load of unsolicited information regarding her failed marriage.

MARTHA: Mitz was my husband's name, but he's dead.

(They both stop laughing.)

[RICK: I am so sorry—]

MARTHA: Actually, he's not really dead, we're divorced. I just prefer to think of him as dead, it's more comforting. *(Realizes)* Oh no! I promised myself I wasn't going to bring up my divorce till later in the evening and I barely even tell you my name and the information's out, the gig is up, you know I'm divorced and there's nothing I can do about it! Damn! So yes, I am divorced. Divorced, divorced, divorced! Does that scare you?

[RICK: Uh, no—]

MARTHA: Oh, I'm so relieved. I just thought maybe you were one of those intense Catholics or something. But actually, can we not even talk about my divorce! I mean, we stood there and swore in front of our 200 closest friends and relatives that we would stay together till death do us part, but neither of us are dead and we have parted so it turns out we lied to our 200 closest friends and relatives! I really should send them all an apology note or something—

[RICK: Anyway, I know this lovely French restaurant down the—]

MARTHA: I'm sorry, Rick, Rick, this is my very first date since my dead husband and I put a stop to the joke that was our marriage,

46

so the last time I was on a date—well, let's see: the guy was wearing bell bottoms and I thought he looked really, really hot. So that gives you an idea of the time frame we're dealing with. Okay? So if I seem a little nervous—do I seem nervous?

[RICK: Oh, no, no—]

MARTHA: You're lying, Rick, I haven't stopped talking since we met, so any idiot could tell I'm very, very nervous. But I appreciate the effort, we're off to a good start.

[RICK: Okay, so this French—]

MARTHA: I've got children, ya know. You hate children, don't you?

[RICK: No!]

MARTHA: Well, I do. I don't hate my children, of course, I hate the concept of having to raise children all by yourself after your husband walks out on your fortieth birthday! Oh my God! I just told you he left me, not visa versa! Oh my God! Damaged-goods alert! Why would her dead husband dump her and run off with an older woman! That's right, Rick, he had a mid-life crisis and he didn't even leave me for someone young and pretty and firm—he left me for a size eighteen with a grandchild and a lisp! So now you're really thinking what is wrong with Martha Mitz! Aren't you, Rick?

[RICK: No, no—]

MARTHA: Well you know what, Rick? I don't care! Cause I believe in myself! I believe I deserve better than my ex-husband! I am the architect of the building which is my life! I'm okay, you're okay! And now, after fifteen years of walking up next to the same

47

LOVE LEMMINGS

unimpressive man, Martha Mitz is ready and in control and wants this goddamn date to start before she loses any of the little nerve she has left and throws up all over Rick Wallace, her very first date since her dead husband left her! I'm scaring you away, aren't I?

LUCY LOVES ME
by **Migdalia Cruz**
Bronx - Present - Cookie (40's)

This one-time beauty queen is slowly going crazy in her apartment as the following monologue reveals.

COOKIE: My nails are dirty. I want red nails.—She won't let me borrow her polish...she should. "It's mine, Momma. Why do you always want everything that's mine?" She should do them for me. Then I can't see the dirt. Don't matter if it's there if I don't see it. That's the kind of hairpin I am. *(SHE goes to the window and sits on the ledge spreading her legs; SHE calls to the people across the way)* Hey, you never saw one like this, did you?! *(SHE comes back into the room)* They never saw this, that's for sure... *(SHE picks up a pair of binoculars and scans the room)* There it is. *(SHE goes to the table, grabs a piece of cheese and puts it in her mouth)* Still good too. There's nothing like a good piece of cheese.—Men could die for this cheese.—I bet cheese could start a war. *(Smiling)* And if it were Swiss cheese, it could be a holy war. *(Laughing raucously)* Oh, dear...I still got it. She don't think I got it, but I got it. *(Long pause)* People who got it know they got it and people who don't, think people who do, don't. But I know. So I got it. *(Pause)* I know she ain't got it.—I want cherry red—no, beet red nails. Deep, deep red. Like someone peeled off my fingernails and the raw red meat shows through.—I'd have to wash my hands more with sores like that. *(Loud music is heard from above; SHE looks up at the ceiling)* Shut up! Shut up! I can't hear myself think! Stupid kids. *(To the ceiling)* Listen to some real music. Let's hear some Satchmo and Ella! *(SHE sings to drown it out)* "In your mountain greenery, where God paints the scenery, just two crazy people together. While you love a lover, let blue skies be your cover. Let—" Shit! I can't do it anymore. I used to sound just like Ella...sometimes I sounded like Billie too. *(Singing)* "My funny valentine...sweet funny valentine...MMmmmhmmmm-hnnn...Is your figure less than Greek? Is your mouth a little weak?

LUCY LOVES ME

When you open it to speak, are you smart? Don't change a hair for me. Not if you care for me...*(SHE continues to sing louder and louder as pounding begins from above and below)* Stay pretty valentine...Stay!" Shut up! Shut up! I can too sing! I'm a professional! *(All the noise stops)* I'm a professional. *(SHE goes to the table and gets her hat and puts it on her head, puts her purse over her arm and moves to the center of the room)* I can't stand it here. No one could. I hate her and I hate this room and I hate my life...I don't know why I called her Lucy. That's my name. Everyone thought it would be cute. Only boys are juniors, I said. I said it would be dumb. I said it was too pretty a name for such an ugly baby. And it was ugly. I'm not just saying that. Believe me. I was there. She didn't have any hair on her head until she was five. Ugly. Ugly, I tell you. Plain ugly.—That's when I changed my name to Cookie.—Who does she think she is anyway?—I'll tell you what she is. She's an ugly little girl who's bad to her mother. She doesn't care if our home smells like the monkey house in the zoo. —I haven't been there in a long time. I don't go anywhere. I don't remember what the Atlantic Ocean looks like.—It probably hasn't changed though. But I'd like to see it again anyway.—She likes the way it smells. She likes everything rotten. Her food tastes rotten. I can't even get a decent piece of cheese around here. One side or the other always has something green on it. She just cuts it off, but me, I can't do that—that's the kind of hairpin I am. *(A bang from below)* I think he robs banks. *(Pause)* Mr. 5K robs banks. Small ones and he keeps the loot stashed in his ceiling under a drop tile. I wonder if he'd murder me if he knew I knew his secret.—I won't tell anyone though, Mr. 5K. I don't snitch. There's honor here. And I'm full of it. Look. *(Reaches into her purse and pulls out a small American flag)* You see. *(Singing)*
"Oh, beautiful, for spacious skies..." *(Loud bang from below)*
He loves it when I sing...Hey, Mister 5K do you play on your piccolo when I sing? I bet you do. I bet you beat your tom-tom for Cookie-Lucy...I coulda done it professionally, know what I mean?

LUCY LOVES ME

I used to always go around singing to myself, and people—people I didn't even know—would come up to me and ask if I was a pro. —It's something the way people pick up on the truth like that. I mean, I wasn't a singer but that's what I always wanted to be. And people just pick that stuff right up, just like that...It's funny, isn't it? I mean, you never know. People always surprise you.

LUSTING AFTER PIPINO'S WIFE
by Sam Henry Kass
A big city - 1989 - Lorraine (30)

Lorraine is a troubled woman who has a hard time relating to people—especially men. Here, she engages in a rather fruit-less session with her therapist.

LORRAINE: I'm just so...I'm just so...So what? Could you help me, here? I'm just so what? Obviously I'm having a little difficulty filling in the blanks—completing the thought process. So you're the doctor. What the fuck am I trying to say? I mean, you are a doctor, aren't you? Do you have a degree? Do you have an answer? Okay, look...I believe all the answers are out there for me. The problem is...The problem has been, that I've failed to recognize them. I'm sure they've all but slapped me in the mouth—And I just don't see it. Do you know what I'm saying? It's one thing not to have any idea what I'm looking for—It's another to realize I'm looking for something, to possibly know what it is, to feel it's there ...Right there...And yet...And yet, what? *(SHE sits up)* What are you, a fuckin' mute? What's the point of all this—To see how many stupid things you can get me to say? You know I'm not making any sense, I know I'm not making any sense, we'll both seemingly never find out, if you have any sense at all... One more thing—I've been meaning to say this for several weeks now...There's a severe odor emanating from your side of the room. It's probably affecting my thought process—Some individuals are highly sensitized to smell. This sort of problem has not received enough publicity in the medical journals...A doctor who stinks—Someone who has a death-like stench about him can bring on some form of mental incapacity in a patient...Sometimes without the patient's knowledge. This is absolutely true. On one hand, please don't take it personally. And on the other hand, you must do something to rectify the problem. No, no...Cracking the window will not solve the problem here. I'm talking about my fuckin' sanity. Do you understand! You must take a shower! You must clean yourself carefully! You are dealing with a human being here. I am not cattle...*(Pause)* Yes...Okay...*(SHE stands up)* See you next week.

LUSTING AFTER PIPINO'S WIFE
by Sam Henry Kass
A big city - 1989 - Lorraine (30)

Lorraine's increasing instability becomes quite evident in her following account of a rather primal encounter with a hunter in a parking lot.

LORRAINE: It was highly romantic...A small diner, right off the Interstate. I was sitting in the corner booth, drinking coffee, picking at some hash browns...There was a tiny jukebox on the table. Peter Lemongello was crooning softly. I glanced out the window and saw a black sedan pull up. On the rooftop, a huge buck was strapped down—Fresh blood was still dripping from the corner of its mouth. The driver's door opened up, and he slid out of the car. He glanced towards the diner, and made eye contact with me through the glass. He smiled seductively, and then ran his filthy hand through his hair. Although we had never talked, I felt completely at ease with him. I got up from my seat, and met him at the front door. He somehow knew I was going to be waiting for him...I suggested we go back to my motel room, and make mad passionate love. He didn't want to wait. He had to have me right then—This I could tell by the look in his one good eye; the other eye I could tell, was fake. That didn't matter to me, though...We got into the back seat of his car, and he unsnapped my jeans. The buck's head was hanging over the side of the roof, and appeared to be watching everything. The whole thing took less than a minute, but I was completely satisfied. I left the car and headed back inside the diner—Suddenly I was hungry. Peter Lemongello was still singing the same song. My lover came in, ordered coffee to go, got back in his car, and drove off...Perhaps forever. If we never meet again, at least we'll always have our moment. *(Pause)* I went back into the woods afterwards, and bagged a couple of squirrels.One shot each. No wasted effort. A clean, quick kill. *(Pause)* So how was your weekend?

MARRIAGE LINES
by Donald Churchill
London - Present - Ruth (40)

When Ruth's husband, Tony, returns home after an evening of drunken revelry, she reveals her fear that he will leave her for a younger woman. When Tony turns the tables by asking her why she never once confessed to a misdeed herself, she offers the following explanation.

RUTH: *(pause then oddly nervous)* You know! I was brought up to think it better for the wife to remain ignorant. Married men do do it...they just do...they did it with me when I was 19. I would have been happy with a husband who misbehaved and never let me know, but that wasn't the husband I got. I knew that if we were going to work, I'd have to sit in the confessional box. I knew that if I let you have your own way in that, you'd let me have my own way in a lot of other more important things. Important to me, that is. Over the years you've told me about...what? Ten women...but they've all been one off...*You* needed to tell me about them...never *quite* sure why. Perhaps the very act of discussing your...little outings...inhibits any chance of emotional involvement with them. You've needed to tell me...I've never had any need to hear it. Frankly, I never like it for a couple of days afterwards...but it makes you happy...so I'm happy. After 20 years with the same person... we've all got to have some safety valve. Yours is a quick one on the office floor. Mine is 9 hours sleep a night. Both weaknesses are a necessary escape.

MARRIAGE LINES
by Donald Churchill
London - Present - Ruth (40)

Ruth's conscience forces her to confess her only marital infidelity in 19 years to her husband Tony. He takes it very well and asks if she enjoyed it. Ruth responds.

RUTH: *(daunted pause)* It was interesting. *(then hastily)* I never thought I *could* do it unless I was emotionally involved. I think that was the main attraction. To see if I could.

[TONY: And you can?]

[RUTH: Yes.] *(BILL appears at the door. They do not see him)* Afterwards I didn't feel a thing...well perhaps a kind of tenderness towards Bill. A little sadness because he's not really very good at it! Despite his reputation. He didn't really make *love* to me...more sort of ransacked me...like a nervous burglar in a jeweller's shop. He's not half so good at it as you.

[TONY: That's always encouraging to hear.]

RUTH: I didn't have a climax...just pretended. *(BILL exits... sadder)* But...it wasn't horrible. The thought of it was very exciting—beforehand. The thought that I was actually going to do it in my own house...on my own sofa made me feel terribly wicked and nervous and excited. I was sorry that it was one of your friends rather than mine, but I know so few men well enough. Those I do I don't fancy. Haven't fancied anyone for years, in fact...'cept you. No, Bill is not really my cup of tea, but I can't wait forever can I? Not when I was 40 last August. I get so few opportunities for meeting men—stuck in the house all day. You must make the best of what opportunities that come your way...mustn't you? You must make your opportunities in this life...don't you think?

OUR OWN KIND
by Roy MacGregor
England - Present - Naila (16)

Following the murder of an Asian in a British council estate,,
the Asian community stages riots and protests. Here, young
Naila shares her feelings on race hatred.

NAILA: They're saying it was my cousin Azam who started the
riot. Don't think he meant to—got carried away by his own rhetoric
as usual. It started as a peaceful demonstration. A protest against
the murder. People were het-up, sure, but it wasn't a howling mob
on the rampage, the way it's being made out. It was when we
reached the Town Hall, and the police tried to turn us back...that
was when the trouble started. That was when Azam leapt up on to
the fountain. He was shouting, 'See, this is what happens when we
try to demonstrate peacefully—they turn us away like sheep!'—I
wrote it all down, I want to do a piece for the school—'They don't
like it when we march together,' he said, 'But when we walk alone
we're attacked and murdered!' That set them all off...and the next
thing you know, the police have charged and all hell's broken loose!
Suddenly the air was full of missiles...bottles and stones...and people
screaming, running in all directions. I ran too—I was terrified! And
then something strange happened. Like an apparition...an old man
standing in the middle of the pavement, lashing out at people with
his walking stick. Caught me one, too. He was shouting: 'This is
England! We don't want any of your woggie nonsense here! Go
home, you scum!' I've never seen such hatred in a face. Azam's
a hothead but he gets people going. The younger boys look up to
him, and even some of the older men secretly approve. I don't
approve, not really. Easy for Azam to shoot his mouth off, it suits
his temperament. Not that he hasn't got a point. Why should we be
humble? Why should we be fearful like our parents? We didn't
arrive here as immigrants. I was born here. I know every tree on
this estate, every brick and every stone, every alleyway and short-
cut. Insider knowledge, that's what I've got. That's what 'home'

56

is: where you know the trees well enough to talk to them...confide in them...tell them your dreams and plans...I try to tell Azam, an ounce of quiet determination...but of course he pays no attention to me. None of them do. I'm just a girl. Might as well be invisible. Well, I won't be invisible forever. One day they'll wake up and they'll see me.

OUR OWN KIND
by Roy MacGregor
England - Present - Lorna (16)

Lorna has been attacked and raped: a brutal reprisal for her father's testimony in a murder trial. Here, the courageous young woman defends her decision to keep the baby that was the result of the racially motivated attack.

LORNA: *(To audience)* There was a time I'd have turned a hose-pipe on those women. But now I'm cool about these things. Live and let live. And that Mrs Elliot...she's been quite kind to me since ...So have other people, in little ways. People *can* be okay some-times. Of course, they all think I'm mentally disturbed. For going ahead with...*(Glances at her stomach)* Even Old Mother Barnes, who's dead against abortion...even she says if anyone had an excuse for it, it's me. But I just smile my new beatific smile and say, 'No thanks, I'll stick with the kid!' I tell them I've missed having a little friend and confident ever since our cat passed on. That raises an eyebrow or two. Of course, there are times when I wonder whether I'm doing the right thing...My counsellor says, 'Don't you think it'll, you know, remind you?' And I say, 'Will an abortion help me forget?' No, they'd have to take my frontal lobes out. *(Pause)* I *do* know what I'm doing. I'm not as touched as they think. I'm going to turn something ugly and vicious into something precious and beautiful! That's what I'm going to do. But Sylvie goes on about its genetic burden. 'Look at the father,' she says. And I say, 'But we don't know him.' 'We know he was a cunt,' she says. And I say, 'No, no; we don't *know* him. We don't know what he might have been if the witch doctors hadn't got hold of him. He might have been a Mozart or a St. Francis!' How can I make them see that I *have* to have this child? Good *has* to triumph over evil. Sylvie says that's just me being a Creeping Jesus as usual. I try to explain it to her...She says, 'Yeah, but any other woman...' And I say, 'Any other woman should be free to choose. *I*, Lorna Howard, choose to have this child!' I *do* know what I'm doing. I do. My child is going to start with a clean slate. It'll be born innocent like we all are, but its smile won't be twisted into a snarl. It won't be asked to pay the debts of its ancestors, or settle old scores. Won't be baptised in blood and told that glory lies in battle. Won't be programmed to storm the battlements, defend the faith, fly the flag... This child is going to have a childhood, full of dreams and fantasies and sunny days and cool waters and warm loving arms! My child will be a recruit to civil peace, not civil war. And when the witch doctors shout 'Gotcha!' they'll be wrong. With one bound, one giant leap for Personkind, my child will be free...free of its shackles ...free of 'our own kind.'

PITZ AND JOE
by Dominique Cieri
Connecticut - Christmas - Present - Pitz (30)

Joe has suffered a traumatic brain stem injury as the result of a
motorcycle accident and is wheelchair-bound. He is able to
leave the institution where he has lived since the accident to
spend Christmas with his family. On Christmas Night, he and
his sister, Pitz, spend the night alone in the house they grew up
in. Here, Pitz shares her memory of the night of his accident.

PITZ: You need a shave, first thing in the morning *(PITZ SITS IN
THE CHAIR BY THE BED.)*
Gee it took you forever to grow hair on your face.
[JOE: *(HE STRUGGLES TO STAY AWAKE)* Forever.]
PITZ: Dad was growing a beard at thirteen. Then he started going
bald at eighteen. So you see it's not so wise to grow a beard so
young, now Dad has no more hair.
"Do I dare and do I dare," how does that go? Something, something
badum, bum, bum... "With a bald spot in the middle of my hair."
You were bald. Well your head was shaved. I thought you were
Dad, honest to God. I had this dream about you the eve of your
accident. *(PITZ STRAIGHTENS OUT THE BED COVERS)* In the
dream I pushed open these doors to a movie theatre. The theatre
was dark and very red, the curtains and the carpet. The theatre was
empty so I walked down the aisle to take my seat, in the first row,
when I heard breathing. Very deep and raspy, very even. I turned
to look and a man was sitting in the first seat in the front row,
against the wall, his head was leaning on the wall. The man's head
was shaved and I knew, I knew it was you and I said out loud, I
said, "Oh it's you Dad, it's you." I said it so loud that I woke
myself up and Colin. I just sat there the rest of the night. The next
day Dad called and said you'd had a motorcycle accident, last rites,
Joe? *(HE IS ASLEEP)* Joe, I got on a plane and when I got to the
hospital I had to walk down this long corridor to get to ICU. I
thought my heart was pounding so loud, I put my hand over my

60

heart to stop the pounding. One great heartbeat echoing off the floors, ceilings, the walls. I pushed open the door to ICU. I heard breathing, respirators forcing life into everyone. I looked for you and there you were in the last bed, in the last row, against the wall and I looked at you and your shaved head and I said, "You look like Dad." You never moved, not for months. I didn't think you would ever wake up, laying there all twisted up with tubes, the left side of your head like a great purple birth mark. How could you have been so careless to get so banged up and so careful not to die?

THE RABBIT FOOT
by Leslie Lee
Rural Mississippi - 1920 - Viola (60's)

When Viola's grandson Reggie returns from fighting in World War I, he reveals to his wife, Berlinda, that he has had an affair with a French woman. Here, Viola tries to comfort Berlinda by sharing a secret from her own past.

VIOLA: Before I give birth to Reggie's mamma—when I was fourteen, fifteen, round there. A young boy, with the bluest eyes I ever seen—white boy that lived in the town. Ev'ry time I passed him by on the street, he'd be watchin' me—not the way other white men looked at me, but like I was the same as him. *(Pause, a clap of THUNDER.)* We tried to stay 'way from one another. It was so hard. Then one day, we met in the woods, and we held onto one another for dear life. And ev'rytime we saw one another, it was like it was the last time. Sneakin' out, layin' in the grass, talkin' 'bout the world the way it shoulda been, and not the way it was. *(Pause, in sorrowful reflection.)* Then, one day, he was dead. Gone from this earth as quick as he came into it. Ridin' a horse. A snake come across his path, and the horse reared up and threw him to the ground, and broke his neck. And I took to the place where we used to meet, and cried where nobody could ask me why I was cryin'.

REEF AND PARTICLE
by Eve Ensler
Here and Now - Reef (20-30)

Reef and Particle's stormy relationship eventually helps to land
Reef in group therapy. Here, she describes her first meeting
with Sexaholics Anonymous.

REEF: I'm the only woman there. The men are mainly old, the
kind you meet in movie theatres at the 4 o'clock in the dark. They
seem really sad. There's one guy who masturbates every 20
minutes. They're nice to me and everything. This guy with pocked
marked skin's talking about girlie pictures and then I realize they're
waiting for me. It's my turn. Oh, hi..., my name's Reef. And I
don't really know if I'm a sexaholic. Particle, he's my boyfriend,
says I'm very sick. So I guess I'm here to find out. Everyone
laughs and then applauds. Particle gives me a really dirty look.

Well, I do think about sex an awful lot and it certainly confuses me,
and it's true I'm never really satisfied. Particle does it so fast, no
introduction, no warning. Just hard. And I do have these ongoing
fantasies. I raise my hand again. Yes. Well. I just want to say
that I'm pretty sure I am a sexaholic. Particle keeps staring at me.
What am I saying? I am a sexaholic. I definitely am. Everyone
applauds. The guy next to me pats me on the head like I've just
taken the vows of the Carmelite nuns. Particle is beaming.
Afterwards he takes me out for lunch at the Oyster Bar. We eat raw
oysters and I imagine doing it with the woman who cuts my hair.
And this deeply comforts me.

F   m

REEF AND PARTICLE
by Eve Ensler
Here and Now - Reef (20-30)

M

F   When Particle knocks at her door after an absence of two years, Reef is reluctant to accept him back into her life. Passion prevails, however, and here Reef addresses her feelings of love to Particle, who is sleeping.

REEF: Boats. Boats and stars. We were going somewhere. We were eating Jordan Almonds. We were sucking the sugar coating in the small boat and we were paddling kind of, splashing and fish were happy and stars and there were no motors. The lake was only the tiny world of our boat and the flashlight on the dark water. The Four Tops singing and your cum inside me.

I'm hot and I'm talking to them again. Talking out, splitting off like my therapist says. I'm hot and I can't take enough off and nothing's protecting me. Run your hands over it. Stay for awhile. Stars. Stars and boats. Is it one person you're always loving? Is it the same person you're loving or trying to love? I am trying to love you Particle. I am always trying to love you Particle and leave you. Inside me. Run Your hands. It's hot. Like poached egg inside me. It could spill out. See my face in it. Almost forming. Almost a face.

SAME OLD MOON
by Geraldine Aron

A convent in Ireland - 1950 - Mother Superior (40-50)
The sexual repression of the 50's combines with the rather
limited views of the Church in the Mother Superior's following
explanation of sexual intercourse.

MOTHER SUPERIOR: *(speaking by rote)* The doughnut represents
the entrance to the female reproductive system, situated down below
and called The Vagina. *(She swings out the doughnut, swings in the
boudoir biscuit.)* The boudoir biscuit represents the exit of the male
reproductive system, also situated down below and called The Penis.
*(She swings out the boudoir biscuit, then brings both items in
slowly.)* Within the holy state of matrimony, the male and female,
wishing to procreate in the name of the Lord, draw together with
lust-free love and chaste thoughts in their hearts. *(She slowly inserts
the end of the boudoir biscuit into the doughnut.)* After a short time
the Lord in His wisdom releases the male seed from the tip of the
boudoir biscuit and causes it to pass through the doughnut in search
of an Egg or Ovum. *(She wiggles the boudoir a little bit. Pause.)*
They say 'tis a beautiful experience. *(Pause)* Nine months later the
fruit of the womb emerges from the doughnut and is baptized as
soon as possible. *(Mother Superior separates the doughnut and
boudoir biscuit, drops them into the open tin, and briskly brushes off
her fingers.)* Is there anything you wish to ask me, Brenda Barnes?
[BRENDA: No Mother.]
MOTHER SUPERIOR: So you now have a complete under-
standing of how Our Lord in his wisdom designed our bodies for
procreation within the blessed bounds of matrimony?
[BRENDA: Yes Mother.]
MOTHER SUPERIOR: Then I'll be on my way. You will meditate
on the wondrous knowledge you have just received. You will not
discuss our meeting with any other girl in the school. And you will
never touch yourself 'down below' except when bathing, at which
time you will avert your eyes and fill your mind with thoughts of the
innocent Virgin Mary. Now you may relax there quietly enjoying
the refreshments. God Bless you, Brenda Barnes.

SAY ZEBRA
by Sherry Coman
Toronto - Present - Javalene (17)

Champion swimmer, Javalene, and Sandra have been best
friends since they were little girls in Toronto. Sandra's idealism
brought her to South Africa where she was arrested and placed
in prison. Javalene risks her own life to find Sandra, and here
reveals her earliest memory of her friend.

JAVALENE: Wherever I am in the city, inside me I'm doing this.
Over and over and over again. Standing on a bus or brushing my
teeth or walking in the rain, inside me I'm moving my arms like
this. Thinking about the one thing that's better than anything else on
the planet—breaking into water from a high dive and getting pulled
into the other world. The place I go to in swimming pools. The
wet forever. Pushing my hands out, pushing the air out in a stream
of bubbles from my nose, feeling the power of my body to move fast
without moving at all. This big blue space all around me, like God.
Stretching longward til the point when I *have* to turn upward.
Finally breaking the surface again, back into the old world, where
she's no longer there. *(stops moving, stares)* The very first time I
ever met Sandra was at Sunnyside Public Pool in Toronto where we
grew up. I was ten and she was almost twelve. I was the one in the
water showing off, she was the one sitting in the bleachers. Sandra
never swam. To her, swimming pools meant sitting in the sun and
melting vanilla ice cream cones all over her body. She did this
because what she really loved to do was lick it all off again. Some-
times I would get so grossed out I'd try to force her in the pool to
wash it off but she was always stronger than me. During that whole
summer and ever since, I only once saw her in the water and that
was in Africa, near Lake Naivasha. In Kenya. I guess it was almost
a year and a half ago now. My head gets dizzy when I try to think
of it. This dizziness is something I feel all the time. I think it's all
my memories floating around my mind with nowhere to go. Getting
tangled up in the waves that come from the other me, the swimmer,
the person who's doing this *(she repeats the stroking movement)*
over and over and over again.

66

SHADES
by Sharman Macdonald
A posh hotel's powder room - Present - Pearl (38)

While on a date, Pearl confronts her reflection in the powder room mirror. Years of loneliness and life as a single parent have taken their toll, as can be seen in the following monologue.

PEARL: Look at that face. That's a terrible face. Fancy waking up every morning to a face like that. What man would want to? Good God I don't want to. What's that look in its eye? I know what you want. I know. You're cheap that's what you are. Aye and you're common too. Do you hear me? Behave yourself. Go home before you do yourself a damage. You've drunk too much. And he's drunk too much. Go home before it ends in tears. *(She gets close to her reflection in the mirror.)* You're not listening to me. Don't you come to me with that face. That's a night face. That face. A 'come to bed' face. You're not going out there with a face like that and you needn't think it. I'll fix you. *(She wipes at her mouth to get the lipstick off. Looks back at the mirror.)* My God you're bold. Look at those eyes. What are you up to eh? Sneaky. What are you going to do eh? Oh my God. You'll do it without me. Murky eyes. I don't trust them. They'll ask for what they want those eyes. No bother. I'll fix that face and you'll not stop me. Anything could happen to a woman that wears a face like that. And none of it nice. It's an open invitation that face. *(She touches the reflection.)* Don't be too obvious. Never put all your cards on the table at once. Do you hear me? Are you listening to me? No man wants a thing if he thinks it's offered to him on a plate. *(Snatches her hand away.)* Take off that face and put a good one on. That's a wicked face. That's the face of a trollop if ever I saw one. *(She washes it at the sink. Looks for a towel.)* Damn. All gone. *(Dries it on the hem of her dress. Looks back at the mirror.)* Pity eh? That's your old Mum's face. Your goody, goody face. Your 'I know what's good for you' face. Your 'I'm telling you' face. A

67

SHADES

Mother's face. That wee bit tired. Strain round the eyes. A bit wan. That's the face that turns your hair white. Nothing'll happen to that face. *(She turns away from the mirror. Looks at her watch. Peers at it.)* You're useless you. Must be late. I'm that tired. I'm that weary. Home to bed that's the thing. Straight home. Straight to bed. Leave the night here. Don't ask for the moon. *(She peeps back over her shoulder.)* Who are you kidding? You'll not fool me and you needn't think it. You're not tired. Not tired at all. You're raring to go, you. *(Takes a decision. Slashes lipstick at her mouth.)* We'll go half way. We've some fun left in us yet and why not? Our life's not over. We've the world in front of us. A half way face. It can take its chance. A 'maybe maybe' face. A bit of lipstick. There's no harm. Nun's eyes and a harlot's mouth. We'll leave it to him. Choice. What do you say Face? He can take his choice. We'll not tell him what we want. Keep him guessing. Eh Face?

SOUTHERN CROSS
by Jon Klein
Rural South - 1850 - Hattie (30's-50's)

Hattie tells of the night she tried to flee across the river in a rowboat to escape slavery.

HATTIE: We got five hours till dawn. *(Billy Daniel jumps down the embankment, with Hattie close behind. They climb into a rowboat and begin to cross the river.)* We was so scared I don't know how we ever got it across. I kept seein' Mr. Tabb with his rawhide or his shotgun, and the current was strong, and I was tremblin' all the way. We didn't dare to say nothin', not even whisper. I jest kept countin' to myself to keep my mind off the fear. Forty-eight, forty-nine, fifty. Then I'd start over again. One, two, three, four, five. I didn't know how far down the river dragged us or how long we'd been gone. I figgured we had to be lost. *(Billy touches her.)* Then Billy sees a light and starts headin' that way. *(A man enters and stands by the light. Suddenly he grabs Daniel and pulls him out of the boat.)* All of a sudden a white man reaches down and grabs him. I start tremblin' all over and tell myself it's time to face the Lord. Then he says something confusin'.

[RANKINS: Howdy folks. You all feelin' hungry? *(Rankins helps Hattie out of the boat.)*]

HATTIE: See, Ohio was a free state, and this white man, John Rankins, operated a free station on the other side of the river. Mr. Rankins told us once you got over the river from Kentucky or Virginia, you could strut all over town as much as you like and no one would bother you.

SPARKY'S LAST DANCE
by Richard Lay
A prison in the South - Present - Nancy (20-30)

A hard-living woman with a thing for ex-cons here tells of her
children and their respective fathers.

NANCY: My three kids call me aunt Nancy because they think my
ma is their ma. I named them all after ice cream flavours. *(Pauses
and smiles)* Peach is my three-year-old son and his daddy is King-
fisher Eddie who's on an oil rig in the Mexican Gulf; then there's
Vanilla, my dear little two-year-old girl whose daddy is Billy Blue,
a Harley Davidson motorcycle mechanic from Houston...and my
little one is Strawberry—she has my red hair and her daddy's black
face...A strange one, that child. But she is as sweet natured as her
father Nutmeg...a lovely man from Mississippi who makes chalk
sticks for schools. All the fathers of my children were convicts...
and, yes I did meet them at Big Ned's bar. Some women go for
rock stars. I like men who've bin prisoners. I don't know why.
They just excite me like nothing else. They come out of jail...and
walk into me.

SPARKY'S LAST DANCE
by Richard Lay
A prison in the South - Present - Lily (20-30)

On the eve of her execution, Lily, an accomplice in murder and robbery, reveals her romantic notions of death by electrocution.

LILY: I've always bin different. I always saw myself as Scarlet O'Hara. I believe dignity and truth are the most worthy assets a woman can have. I used to dream about how dignified and truthful I could be. Pa died early, no fault of his own—he just gave up when he couldn't pay the bills...Ma still mends sewing machines in New Orleans. She always loved Hurricane more than she cared for me. It's tough not being loved...On St. Valentine's Day I always send myself 10 cards and pray for an 11th...It never comes. It never will. Won't be long now Nancy. My gas and your injection. Hurricane chose Sparky I read. He was making a statement. The last man to be executed in an electric chair.

[NANCY: He always was a show-off. Sparky's Last Dance. Thinka that.]

LILY: *(romantically)* Sparky's Last Dance. Will it be quick for him? Will it be a waltz or a tango? Will it be a rap or a rumba. ...Or will his head fry and his eyes pop out *(laughs)*. 'Aint I awful..

71

THE SUBSTANCE OF FIRE
by Jon Robin Baitz
New York City - Present - Marge Hackett (50-60)

Marge Hackett is a social worker and the widow of a dishonest politician who committed suicide. She visits Isaac Geldhart, a shut-in at his home, where she had been to a cocktail party years earlier when Isaac was riding high. He asks her to dinner and when she declines, Isaac asks if she is waiting for a better deal and how many more chances she thinks she has.

MARGE: I'm not waiting for anything. In the last five years I put myself through school and got this job, which, admittedly is not what I imagined, but still. What have you *done*, lately? I have a child. I had to drive out to Long Island with a suit for my husband, because he was wearing jogging pants and a Drexel Burnham tee-shirt when they found him. *(Pause)* Chance? Fuck you. Chance? Man, I hope I don't look fragile or give the impression that I'm on some sort of widow's walk. I have a son who knows his father ripped off everything in this city that wasn't nailed down! I watched my husband on news at five, *weeping*. Chance? What chance do I have? Because I won't have dinner with you? Look at you! Back then you wouldn't look at me, except for a laugh at my husband's expense, and now you want dinner because we've both been flattened? *(Beat)* Do you know how much I hate having dinner by myself night after night? Well, I'd rather do that, let me assure you, than have dinner with you and compare bad-break notes.

THE SUMMER THEY STOPPED MAKING LUDES
or How Taking Peyote Turned Me Into A Coyote
by Steven Tanenbaum
Poolside, suburbia - 1970's - Eve (17-20)

When Monique and Eve share memories of their adolescent
sexual exploits, Eve reveals that she was pregnant when she was
13.

EVE: I never told anybody. I was only thirteen. Yeah, I'm thirteen years old and I've got to visit the gynecologist so some fat, bald
guy can stick his pudgy fingers inside me. The guy fits me for an
IUD so I won't ever have to worry again. Right. Next thing I
know, I'm in the hospital for a D and C. I'm thirteen years old so
what the hell do I know from those kind of things. Like what's a D
and C—"Dusting and Cleaning." Yeah, "Dusting and Cleaning," I
recommend that every woman have her uterine walls scrubbed clean
with a scouring pad. Okay, so they put me on the pill which was
great until I became so bloated I started to resemble Marlon Brando
in the *Godfather*—mustache included. So they take me off the pill
and give me a diaphragm. A device that was invented to take all
spontaneity out of sex. I never know when's the right time to put it
in. I mean, half the time I put it in and nothing happens. And it's
not till the next day, when I'm talking to someone about the weather
that I remember I've still got Mickey Mouse's trampoline stuck up
my crotch. Lately, I've dispensed with all the modern forms of
contraception. You see, I've developed my own method of birth
control: Move to Colorado. I know that all I have to do is get out
of here and everything will be all right.

THE SUMMER THEY STOPPED MAKING LUDES
or How Taking Peyote Turned Me Into A Coyote
by Steven Tanenbaum
Poolside, suburbia - 1970's - Monique (15-20)

Monique is romantically pursued by Art, a young man into peyote. When she finally agrees to go out with him, they wind up talking in the moonlight. As Art trips, Monique weaves a tale of her childhood for him.

MONIQUE: I assure you, you will be disappointed because it is a very ordinary tale. But since you asked...When I was three years old, my parents decided to move out of the city because they felt it was no place to raise a child. My father had a brother who lived out west and they decided to go into business together so my family moved into this sprawling ranch house just on the edge of some new development that was under construction at that time. Not too long after we moved there, my mother got into the habit of putting me in the backyard to play while she puttered around in the house. From our backyard, you could look in any direction and see miles and miles of unrestricted desert. Well, on this one particular day, I think I was drawing pictures in the earth with a stick when I looked up and saw a coyote standing in front of me. Since I had never seen a coyote before, I mistook it for a dog and began to pet it. Now, the coyote must have heard some noise because he reared as if he were going to leave. So I asked the dog if he would like to stay in my house and be my pet. Well, the coyote was very flattered by my offer but he said that he must return to the desert because it was not safe for him to be so far away from home. If I liked, however, the coyote said he would take me to a place where we could play to our heart's content. I told him it would be all right as long as I was back before dark. I did not want to worry my mother needlessly. So the coyote picked me up by my cheek and carried me off into the desert to play with all the coyotes. And everyday after that, I'd wake up and rush out to the backyard where the coyote would be waiting to take me into the desert. Now, the strange thing about all

74

THE SUMMER THEY STOPPED MAKING LUDES

this was that everyday he would bite down on my cheek, pick me up and carry me away in his jaws; and when he would do this, I could feel the warm blood trickling down my cheek. But when I returned home each night, the wound would be completely healed and my parents never suspected a thing. Until this day, no one has ever noticed my scar. All my mother ever said to me was that if I continued to spend all my time playing outside, I'd become so dark people would mistake me for an Indian. So everyday, for seven years, the coyote took me into the desert. Then after I had turned ten, my father decided to move the family back east. When I told the coyote I was leaving, he told me not to be sad because everything I saw and learned would always be with me. I hugged the coyote and we both cried. Then without a word, the coyote bounded off and disappeared into the desert. The next day I moved to a place where there is no horizon; where there is no desert; and where there is no coyote...That's the story of how I received my scar. I told you it would be boring.

TALKING THINGS OVER WITH CHEKHOV
by John Ford Noonan
New York City - Present - Marlene (20's-30's)

Marlene runs into her ex while jogging in the park. Some of the
old feelings surface, both good and bad. He asks her about the
man she now lives with. She replies.

MARLENE: We have a life based on mutual sharing.
[JEREMY: It's obviously working. You've never looked better.]
MARLENE: When we first get up, he gives me a hug and says,
"Hi, BEAUTIFUL, HERE'S ANOTHER DAY." For Herbert it's
not a line. It's what he really feels. Herbert's full of feeling. He
calls me from work every day around two, no matter what.
[JEREMY: Suppose you feel like going out?]
MARLENE: He brings me flowers. He surprises me with presents.
He's always leaving me notes under my pillow. He calls when he's
going to be late. No matter what, we're together every weekend.
He remembers the little things.
[JEREMY: They all sound pretty big to me.]
MARLENE: That's what he's always saying: "ONLY IF BOTH
PARTIES REMEMBER THE LITTLE THINGS CAN LOVE GET
BIG." He's everything I've always wanted.
[JEREMY: Everything I could never be.]
MARLENE: He never leaves his clothes around. He never farts...
at least not in front of me. He never picks between his toes and
smells it. He never sits playing with his balls. He doesn't need
girlie magazines. He's beyond talking dirty. There's nothing with
batteries in his drawer.
[JEREMY: That was only toward the end.]
MARLENE: He does the dishes. Shares the shopping. Oh sweet
Jesus, can you hear it in my voice?!
[JEREMY: What?]
MARLENE: I'm as angry at you as the day I threw you out.

THE TATTLER
The Story and Stories of a Pathological Liar
by Terri Wagener
Here and Now - Glad Aggy (12)

When Glad Aggy's family gathers for dinner, they are treated to
an extra special performance of the 12-year-old's storytelling
skills as she spins an outrageous yarn of the Scandal at the
Babies' Hospital.

GLAD AGGY: Didn't it mention the terrible scandal over at the
Babies' Hospital?

[FATHER: *(Carefully.)* Not that I recall.]

[GLAD AGGY: *(Shaking her head as others exchange looks.)* It's
over and beyond my comprehension.]

[CANDY: Where is the Babies' Hospital?]

[GLAD AGGY: Out on the way out of town. Out way out past city
limits. Out where Jesus lost his sandals.]

[CANDY: That's a strange place for a Babies' Hospital.]

[GLAD AGGY: It's so people in town don't have to hear the
pregnant people screaming.]

However, I heard it last night, I did. Me and Ooopalee and my
imaginary friend named Wally—we heard the screams so loud I
jumped right out of my skin—

[CANDY: What happened?]

GLAD AGGY: —the very excitement chapped my lips. Chapped
my whole body.

[MOTHER: *(Staring wild-eyed at GLAD AGGY, speaking to
FATHER.)*
Dear…]

[FATHER: Tell your mother what happened, Aggy.]

GLAD AGGY: *(Takes a breath and begins a story.)* Armageddon
Sawyer was giving birth to a wee one and bellowing like a prune fed
calf. Me and Ooopalee and my imaginary friend named Wally were
out catching lightning bugs and turning them into diamond rings.
Then the sky began descending black and white, not blue, and I

77

heard the screaming where I was and hurried over to the delivery room.

[CANDY: Go on.]

GLAD AGGY: Armageddon Sawyer was yelling like nobody's business, and I pride myself on having a great sense of event. *(Referring slightly to ROGER.)* Some may not be able to appreciate that.

[CANDY: What happened next?]

GLAD AGGY: I snuck my way down the long white corridor which was shaking with her breathing and screaming and sobs. Then I pushed on the door of the delivery room and ducked behind a Windsor rocking chair they have there in the corner. Across the room was Armageddon Sawyer tossing her cookies on a Chesterfield sofa.

[ROGER: *(Snorts.)* A Chesterfield sofa?]

[GLAD AGGY: *(Perfectly serene.)* A Chesterfield sofa.]

[ROGER: *(Mutters.)* I wish I was as cocksure of anything as she is of everything.]

[CANDY: *(To GLAD AGGY.)* And?]

GLAD AGGY: And nothing. Just nothing. I pulled out a recent copy of the Reader's Guide to Periodical Literature and commenced to read to myself.

[CANDY: But what about Armageddon?]

GLAD AGGY: *(Nods.)* She was there. Stripped naked. Belly blown up. Perspiration coming out of her pores in little fluttering stars. They had her by a window and the moon was shining on her face, pulling it out of shape. *(Aside to Candy.)* Never sleep in the moonlight, remember. It'll pull your face right over— *(She demonstrates, then is immediately back in the story.)* I myself was struck all of a heap. Pain skittered up from my legs to my chest and across my shoulders. I couldn't catch my breath from pure compassion for Armageddon...

[CANDY: I understand.]

[GLAD AGGY: *(Pauses and touches her gently.)* You understand the most interesting things.]

(Immediately back into the story.) I experienced a dizzy spell and then clutched right here at my pill pocket. *(Hand to heart. Aside to CANDY—)*

Here I carry three little pill bottles containing grains of wheat from the Holy Land, water from the Jordan and Dead Sea, and earth from the Mount of Olives. Better than nitroglycerine.

(Back to story.) I began to feel faint—but I faint so slowly that I never hit the floor before the scandal came about. *(Pause.)*

[MOTHER: What?]

[CANDY: What happened?]

GLAD AGGY: Armageddon's father pounded his way into the place, yelling louder than she was, even. "Quit yer belly-achin'!" he was thundering around. The skin on his face looked like blistered paint, and he has yellow goat whiskers coming out of his chin. He had a blue jay feather growing from behind one ear and he tore at his shirt as he went around, so it came off in rags hanging off him, his hair belly sticking out like a beaver's home.

All the doctors and nurses stared at him. And me, too, I did. Like the people looked at Medusa before she turned them into stone, I expect. And then he stood very still and huge, his eyes glittering like two bright chips of green bottle glass. And he let out a scream and flapped up and down his arms and darted about the room shooing all the doctors and nurses.

Everybody ran out but me behind the rocking chair. It got so quiet I could hear my throat swallow, and little gnats were hovering around my heart. Mr. Sawyer turned to his daughter and growled real low, "Now sweat, you bitch hound!"

[CANDY: What'd she do?]

GLAD AGGY: She sweat. It poured off her. First it came in little rivulets, shining clear and silver. Then it flowed to the ends of her blueberry blonde hair and made a little puddle underneath where she was lying. And her daddy was pacing around in circles and pulling up his shoulders and shaking his head like a crazy man. He talked about how he loved her and she didn't want to hear about it. He talked about the night they had done the Sexual Intercourse so she could give birth to a husband. *(Pause.)*

[CANDY: *(Closing one eye.)* Do what?]

GLAD AGGY: She'd have a baby and get him young and treat him rough and train him right and marry him when he could toddle and have the ideal husband.

[CANDY: Oh.]

[MOTHER: Oh my.]

GLAD AGGY: *(Nods.)* Scared the holy sugar outta me. And Armageddon was pushing and straining and crying and Mr. Sawyer was yelling and pacing and shaking and every once in a while he turned his head and spat on the floor behind where he walked. Then the blood streaked out from Armageddon's bottom and her daddy let it drip and fall into the sweat and spit on the floor.

(CANDY DISCREETLY PUSHES HER PLATE AWAY.)

The thing was born and they screamed together in ecstasy and it shot across the room and bounced on the opposite wall and ricocheted back to the daddy's waiting arms.

And I stood up and peeked through the rocker slats thinking I too would one day do this dazzling, this beautiful, this utterly impossible thing, and then I saw the thing looked just like a Mr. Potato Head. It had a teeny weeny little body and a big monster face with no eyes and a hollering blue and green mouth.

Mr. Sawyer dropped it and it roared like a demon and Mr. Sawyer ran out in the hall for help and came back and tried to beat it to death with a cat he'd found. All the doctors rushed in to operate and a clumsy-fingered she-bear came down the hall, stuck her head in the door and said, "What, no peanuts?" and then she went back on outside and Armageddon started breathing more regular.

[CANDY: *(In a breathless whisper, after a pause.)* Did they save it?]

GLAD AGGY: They performed open heart surgery on its tiny little chest. And as soon as they cut a hole in it, the heart burst wide, and thousands of little black sparrows flew out...

Through the windows and over the rooftops and out into the big...night...sky...

(HER VOICE TRAILS OFF WITH THE IMAGE. THE OTHERS SIT SILENT, MESMERIZED. GLAD AGGY STANDS SLOWLY, LIKE A QUEEN, AND OFFERS HER HAND TO CANDY.)

GLAD AGGY: God bless you with peace and love and glory.

(SHE SHAKES CANDY'S LIMP HAND, THEN APPROACHES ROGER AND LEANS TO HIM.)

GLAD AGGY: It's better than real talk, isn't it?

(SHE FLOUNCES OUT, LEAVING THE OTHERS FROZEN, LOST IN STORY AND THOUGHT.

LIGHTS FADE TO BLACK.

END OF SCENE ONE.)

THE TATTLER
The Story and Stories of a Pathological Liar
by Terri Wagener
Here and Now - Glad Aggy (50)

The years haven't served to diminish Glad Aggy's penchant for embellishment as can be seen in her interpretation of the crucifixion and resurrection of Jesus.

GLAD AGGY: You got the story from the Bible, I guess. *(DOCTOR shrugs innocently.)*
A collection of stories made up by different people who talk about seeing various things happen or of hearing about these things from people whose relatives were alive at the same time that some other people heard these stories and told them at parties. *(DOCTOR nods, WOMAN gasps with horror.)*

(GLAD AGGY takes a breath and then continues.)   The Bible tells me that, mostly, in the beginning, God was a very good hater. Mad and bad and dangerous to know. He yelled a lot and tore his hair. He did not take correction well, and had, shall we say, questionable taste. *(WOMAN gasps even more loudly.)*   Get him on an off day and he could send people screaming into the night. I tell you, if he rose on the wrong side of the bed, well, he talked only to people he felt like talking to, and rarely discussed the situation fully before he tossed his lightning.   Regular fits this God thought up and threw down—frogs falling out of the sky, flies and lice and rain and hail, unsightly rashes and open, running sores—

(NURSE HAS BEEN WRITING ALL THIS DOWN.   SHE FRANTICALLY TURNS THE PAGE OF HER CLIPBOARD AND CONTINUES WRITING.   GLAD AGGY PAUSES, AND SMILES CONSPIRATORIALLY WITH DOCTOR.)

GLAD AGGY: I like to think this God was a very young God. Some younger children are allergic to most everything, you know.

THE TATTLER

(GUS nods seriously at this medical fact.) Makes them unpleasant all day long... *(Pause.)*

BUT...what great stories came out of these God times. *(WOMAN prepares to faint.)*

The best of them is Jesus. Jesus, it seems, was the sort of person who if he walked past someone trying to parallel park, would stop and direct traffic. *(WOMAN begins to breathe heavily.)* He was a very fine man. God gloats upon such a man. His Christianity was muscular. He'd step out of a community shower to pee. *(WOMAN yelps.)* I like Jesus. I'd like to have him over for dinner...if he weren't dead.

(THE WOMAN IS HAVING A FIT. DOCTOR NODS TO HER SLIGHT AND SPEAKS TO NURSE.)

[DOCTOR: Nurse.]

(SHE NODS AND STEPS OFFSTAGE, RETURNING IMMEDIATELY WITH PARAMEDICS. THEY CARRY WOMAN OFF, SHE TWITCHES SPASMODICALLY. DOCTOR LOOKS TO GLAD AGGY. HE THEN PICKS UP THE STRAIT JACKET AND TOSSES IT AFTER THE WOMAN.)

[DOCTOR: Pardon the interruption. Continue.]
GLAD AGGY: [Well, there's not much to continue.] There is a story, however, that pretty early on a Friday morning, Jesus was assassinated by bears.

[NURSE: Bears?]
[DOCTOR: Bears.]
GLAD AGGY: They stripped him naked and dragged him up a hill wearing nothing but bracelets and crowns of ironweed and sun-

flowers. And they put him high up in a tree with cats and white blossoms and told him he couldn't come down. The sky was a soft and rainy blue and the east was a smoky gold, and the air was as purple as violet wisterias, and the crowd was a bunch of big black bears. *(NURSE looks up from writing, then returns to it quickly.)*

Jesus sat up there thinking maybe he'd made a mistake. Wondering who was right and what did it matter, who knew best and what were the questions to the answers. Pain skittered up from his legs to his chest and across to his shoulders and his back, grown broad and curved like the shell of a turtle. And his gullet started aching and his skeleton was trembling, tears salting his eyes, and he thought he was probably too old for all this. His own red heart went boom boom boom.

By and by, his heart outgrew his thoughts and burst through his chest with a sound like water and thousands of tiny black sparrows filled the sky from noon till after three.
(Pause. NURSE turns a page.)

Jesus let out a cry to curdle blood—to shake whole kingdoms—and all the white flowers fell off the tree. Eternity was in that moment. Jesus Christ screamed to the sky, "Let me in. God, I'm finished with praying." And he disappeared. The desert was left muttering and making noises.

(THERE IS A LONG PAUSE. NURSE LETS OUT A LONG BREATH, MOVED. DOCTOR WAITS, THEN SELF-CONSCIOUSLY WIPES HIS EYES AND FACE.)

GLAD AGGY: *(Brighter.)* Then, three days later, Jesus reappeared, awakened by his own groan. He set his mind to enumerating all the beds of his life in an effort to discover where he was. Then Jesus Christ gasped with astonishment. He gathered a crowd and said to them all, "I told you so."

THE TATTLER

(ANOTHER PAUSE. NURSE REPLACES PAGES ON CLIPBOARD SLOWLY. DOCTOR PACES AWAY SLIGHTLY, THEN TURNS BACK TO GLAD AGGY, STUDYING HER.)

GLAD AGGY: *(LOOKS BACK AT HIM, SITS UP VERY STRAIGHT.)* I say Jesus was quite the right sort of thing. Nobody saw that he was trying to do something quite different. They merely thought he was trying to do the usual thing, and had not succeeded very well...

(DOCTOR WATCHES HER, STANDS UP STRAIGHT, AND POINTS TO HER SLOWLY, THE OTHER HAND TRAVELING TO TOUCH HIS NOSE. NURSE CLOSES HER CLIPBOARD. GLAD AGGY RELAXES, GRINS AT DOCTOR, AND SWINGS HER LEGS HAPPILY.)

TELLING TALES
by Migdalia Cruz
Here and Now - Woman (30-40)

SAND - Here, a woman shares the horrific memory of the death
of her sister.

SAND: She wasn't supposed to go on the roof. I tole her not to.
But she wouldn't listen to me. She never listens to me. She's
always the brave one.

I cried for a long time after that. I cried for her and I cried for
me, because I din't go with her. I din't know what was gonna
happen. And now I'll always wonder what woulda happened if I'da
gone.

I was on the fire escape when they caught him. A whole army
of men from the neighborhood were carrying him up above their
heads. And he squirmed like a rat, like a fucking rat in a corner
surrounded by hungry cats.

They took him into the playground and threw him down into the
sandbox. Everybody stood around him and screamed at him. You
couldn't even understand what they were saying.

I closed my eyes for a minute and when I opened them again, he
was buried in the sand. Two men held him down while everybody
else threw sand in his face. His eyes were filled with it and he was
screaming. Then they filled up his mouth and the screaming stopped. He threw up and choked and he kept choking on his own blood
and spit and sand.

And I smiled...

That's when I thought there must be a God, because there was
justice.

They picked him up and my daddy tied his legs to the back of
his '58 Plymouth Valiant. He got that car the day I was born—two
months before Anita was born. That car was us. It was as old as
us. Eight years old. So wise for eight. So strong. Stronger than
we could ever be. Stronger than my father. They dragged him
through the streets he knew so well. The streets we played in.

TELLING TALES

Where he watched us and made his plan. I hoped that car would climb to the roof and jump over—like Anita. Rip him up, like he ripped Anita. Take his hands and make him pull his own guts out. And then the balls. Slash. Cut. Tear.

He tore her clothes off with his teeth. He ripped her open with his teeth. His teeth were yellow and sharp—like gold. Golden teeth. Now he had vomit and blood caked onto his teeth. They weren't so pretty like they used to be. They looked good now. Like they were supposed to look.

We keep away from the sandbox now. It's strange when people from an island are scared of sand.

TELLING TALES
by Migdalia Cruz
Here and Now - Woman (30-40)

RATS - Having made the move from the South Bronx to suburban Connecticut, a woman finds it difficult to let go of some of the more extreme elements of her past.

RATS: He says violence isn't the answer. They're just looking for a warm place to live out the winter, and in the spring they'll be gone. But I hear them. In the walls. In the drawers. Everyday I check the flour for them. They get everywhere. He says we shouldn't kill them. That won't keep them from coming back. He's a scientist, so he knows. He also says how can you kill anything that's so cute.

"But they ate all my sweet corn and my marigolds and my squash seeds," I say. "We can buy more," he says. I say, "Why should we have to?" I say, "They're aliens, invaders. Get the hell out of my seeds and grains." I'm not a monster. I'm willing to give them my thyme. It's all dried up now anyway, but there's plenty of it. And it's right there in the front yard. Right where they can get their grimy little teeth on it. But no. They gotta come inside my house.

I never liked mice. The ones in my parents' apartment were gray—baby rats really. Nobody cared about the souls of those guys. They were dirty, ugly and smelled like urine, other animals' urine—not even their own urine, you know what I mean? City mice are nobody's friends. You kill city mice. You don't gently catch them in Hav-A-Heart traps and release them into some pretty country field. There are no fields so if you let 'em go they will a) Come back or b) bite you and give you rabies. So you have no choice. You use those lovely, backbreaking snap traps. By doing this, you prevent disease, death, desolation. You keep little rats from becoming big rats that will eat small children.

My father caught rats at work. They had contests to see who could catch the biggest one. The danger, of course, was that the rat might break out of the plastic bag it was caught in and rush the crowd of laughing men, throwing down their dollar bills in drunken bets. The rats usually lost.

There was this one guy—Paco Loco—my dad says Dominicans will do anything for money—who was offered twenty dollars to catch a rat with his bare hands and strangle it. Paco went after a big one, but he slipped when he got right up to it and had cornered it. As he grabbed for it, the rat jumped smack into his face, bit him and kept running past the other men who all ran screaming out the door. My dad was the only one who stayed. He says the rat stopped and looked at him. He said it looked scared. Imagine that. Even with blood hanging off his teeth, he was still scared of people. Then he kept right on going, under the steel machinery, disappearing into the wall. My dad went over to Paco and helped him up. Paco was crying. The rat got his left eye. I mean, it was completely gone. It was just a hole.

They stopped playing with the rats after that.

I thought I left those things behind me. In the Bronx. But they followed me here. To white suburbia. I'm the only Puerto Rican in New Canaan, Connecticut. I figure as long as I don't open my mouth I'm safe. I was at a party once and some WASPY lady in tennis whites asked if I was from England. England?! Can you imagine?! She said she thought I was from England because I had an accent. She looked real surprised when I told her I was from the South Bronx. "South what?" But once she got used to the idea, it seemed quite wonderful and she grabbed my elbow and brought me around to all of her friends. "Have you met this wonderful creature, yet? She's from the Bronx—the South Bronx!" "Amazing! Is anybody still living there?" No—nobody important...just people. My mother, my father, my sisters. The priest who gave me first communion. My friend Sharon whose little brother Junie died of sickle cell anemia when we were twelve and he was ten. She's a cop now. I bet she's a good cop. Forty-fourth precinct. Otherwise known as Fort Apache. It's funny...when I lived there it seemed more like Fort Navajo or Fort Chippewa. My people are a peaceful people. It's when they herd us into barrios that we turn—like a rat in a plastic bag. When you're fighting for your life, you get ugly. You get bitter. Or if you're like my mother, you spend a lot of time in church lighting candles. And you bring your children with you so they forget for a time that they've been forsaken.

The church is beautiful. It smells wonderful. It smells purple, like a purple, powerful drug. I loved the church. When I was sixteen I decided to become a part of the church. You know, settle down, get married to the Son of God. But it didn't work out too well. I liked to read too much. And I liked to write. Mother Superiors don't like that kind of stuff. After three weeks, four days, nine hours, I left. I think my mom was disappointed. Back to the Bronx. Wasn't any one of us going to get out? The Bronx—where people talk with such intriguing accents.

He doesn't understand why they upset me so much. With their cute little noses and big, brown eyes. They look just like his eyes. Just like mine. But they squeak, I don't squeak, do I? Maybe I do. Maybe I shouldn't be afraid of them, but I am. The scuttling sounds behind the wall remind me. I wonder if what they say is true—that you have the memories of all your ancestors inside your head. I wonder if my children will jump when they hear mice in the walls. I wonder if they'll remember too and get up in the middle of the night to check on people who aren't there anymore...

Maybe he's right. Maybe it's time to put away the knife.

UNCHANGING LOVE
by Romulus Linney
Manard, North Carolina - 1921 - Judy (15-18)

Judy is sold by her parents to the well-to-do Benjamin Pitman, who wants her to marry his eldest son and provide him with grandchildren. When Judy's son is murdered by Leena, the jealous wife of Benjamin's younger son, Judy brings his body to Benjamin to say goodbye.

JUDY: I will ask you to get Tommy a coffin and to dig his grave. *(Benjamin nods.)* And I will ask you to buy a small stone with his name on it and put it there. *(Benjamin nods.)* And I will ask you to let me go back to my mother and my father and not be married to Shelby no more. *(Benjamin nods.)* I won't be bitter. Tommy wouldn't want that. I will do what he'd like, someday, have a sister for him, a brother, too, maybe. And when we see each other again, if I have something to eat, I will give it to you, and hope you will want it. You won't need it. Barbara will cook your food for you. Leena will run your store and the brick factory will do good. You'll get richer, and we'll get poorer. But I hope you will stop when you see me, and if I have some- thing for you, you will take it. *(A simple phrase on a guitar. Lights fade.)*

WALKING THE DEAD
by Keith Curran
Boston - Present - Dottie (50's)

Conservative Dottie has agreed to attend a memorial gathering
for her daughter—a transsexual—hosted by Maya, her daughter's
lover. Here, Dottie reveals her anger and grief.

DOTTIE: Alright, I've decided to talk about how being a mother in
times like these can be utterly dispiriting. Declarations of just about
anything can happen—primarily on visits for Christmas and Thanksgiving. It seems that children see holiday visits as the ideal times to
get all serious and confessional. I dread these times. Not only
because Veronica told me she was moving out one Christmas, leaving school that New Years, that she resented me for her father's
death a few Thanksgivings before that, and that she was a lesbian
one subsequently horrifying Easter Sunday—but that all of my girl-
friends call up around the holidays to cry over what *their* children
dropped in their laps that holiday visit. Leona's son, Hal, used a
Thanksgiving to suddenly be a lifelong alcoholic, and Debbie
Monahan's oldest daughter, Sheila, told her she was impregnated
with a stranger's sperm the following Fourth of July. Labor Day
Christina's twins *both* revealed they were involved in ethical
scandals at the workplace, and one Christmas Eve was all about
Colleen's son, Leonard, who had recently decided to leave a very
successful accounting firm and become a choreographer. Well, I've
gone on far longer than was suggested, but I wanted to explain how
the decorations going up on Chestnut Street can make a mother start
screaming in her sleep.

93

PERMISSIONS ACKNOWLEDGMENTS

LOVE DIATRIBE by Harry Kondoleon. © Copyright, 1990, by Harry Kondoleon. Reprinted by permission of the author's agent, George P. Lane, William Morris Agency, 1350 Avenue of the Americas, New York, NY 10019.

LOVE LEMMINGS by Joe DiPietro. © Copyright, 1991, by Joe DiPietro. Reprinted by permission of the author.

LUCY LOVES ME by Migdalia Cruz. © Copyright, 1987, by Migdalia Cruz. Reprinted by permission of the author's agent. For a copy of the play, please send $5 and a SASE to Peregrine Whittlesey, 345 East 80th Street, New York, NY 10021.

LUSTING AFTER PIPINO'S WIFE by Sam Henry Kass. © Copyright, 1990, by Sam Henry Kass. Reprinted by permission of the author.

MARRIAGE LINES by Donald Churchill. © Copyright, 1991, by Donald Churchill. Reprinted by permission of the author's agent, Gordon Dickerson, Peters Fraser and Dunlop, 5th Floor, The Chambers, Chelsea Harbour, Lots Road, London, SW10 OXF, England.

OUR OWN KIND by Roy MacGregor. © Copyright, 1990, by Roy MacGregor. Reprinted by permission of the author and his agent. Applications for permission to perform OUR OWN KIND by Roy MacGregor should be made in advance to Curtis Brown, 162-168 Regent Street, London W1R 5TB, England (Attention: Sebastian Born) in writing or by fax to 011-4471-872-0332.

PITZ AND JOE by Dominique Cieri. Copyright registration number 8198627. Reprinted by permission of the author.

THE RABBIT FOOT by Leslie Lee. Copyright © 1991 by Leslie Lee. Reprinted by permission of the author's agent, Ellen Hyman, 422 East 81st Street, #4C, New York, NY 10028.

REEF AND PARTICLE by Eve Ensler. © Copyright, 1990, by Eve Ensler. The play was first produced at Home for Contemporary Theatre and Art, 1990. Reprinted by permission of the author.

SAME OLD MOON by Geraldine Aron. © Copyright, 1991, by Geraldine Aron. Reprinted by permission of the author's agent. Acting edition published by Samuel French Ltd., UK. For professional performing rights apply to Alan Brodie Representation, 91 Regent Street, London W1R 7TB, England.

SAY ZEBRA by Sherry Coman. Copyright © 1990 by Sherry Coman. All rights reserved. CAUTION: Professionals and amateurs are hereby warned that "Say Zebra" is subject to a royalty. It is fully protected of all countries covered by the International Copyright Union